About the author

An experienced IT lecturer, Jackie is the author of Age Concern Books' bestselling title *Getting the Most from Your Computer*, which is now in its second edition. She is also a regular contributor to IT problem pages in magazines and Websites aimed at the over 50s. Jackie is based in Abingdon, Oxfordshire.

EVERYDAY COMPUTER ACTIVITIES

a step by step guide for older home users

JACKIE SHERMAN

Published by Age Concern England
1268 London Road
London SW16 4ER

First published 2005

Editor Ro Lyon
Production Leonie Farmer
Design and typesetting GreenGate Publishing Services, Tonbridge, Kent
Printed in Great Britain by Bell & Bain Ltd, Glasgow

A catalogue record for this book is available from the British Library

ISBN-13: 978-0-86242-403-9
ISBN-10: 0-86242-403-8

Contents

Contents

Introduction

Many people own a computer but don't use it very much, if at all. Perhaps you are in this position: you may not be aware of its possibilities, or you may have found it too difficult to learn how to use properly. Fortunately, things don't have to stay this way.

This book will take you step by step through many of the activities that older people find useful when they start using their computer at home, including working with a digital camera or scanned pictures; playing games; Internet shopping; producing labels; sending photos via email; comparing prices; and creating greetings cards.

Following these activities will help you overcome any reluctance you might have in using your machine, and show you how easy it can be to get the most from your computer.

Nearly all the examples in the book are based on computers running the Windows XP operating system and Microsoft Office 2002 (Office XP) programs, but you will find the screens look very similar if you are running Windows 98, 2000 or ME and the projects will work equally well with earlier versions of Microsoft Office.

The screenshots (for example, of the Baby Boomer Bistro on pages 113–115) were taken winter 2004–2005. You may notice some changes on Websites since then.

If you don't have a basic knowledge of computers, including using the mouse and working with windows, turn to the Appendix first of all for a brief introduction. There is also a Glossary to explain technical terms.

Throughout the book, menu options are shown in **bold** type.

Word processing

Most people who use a computer start by trying their hand at word processing. Letters, invitations and articles look so much more professional, and can be quickly amended and saved.

Starting work

Open your word-processing application by clicking the Word icon ▥ on the Office Shortcut Bar or by selecting **Microsoft Word** from the **Start – All Programs** menu (see Figure 1.1).

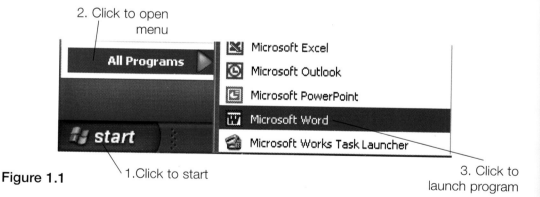

Figure 1.1

Whenever Word opens, it displays a blank page ready for you to start typing. To begin a second piece of work, click the **New** toolbar button you will see on the toolbar at the top of the screen ▯ . Note that only commonly used toolbar buttons will be visible on any toolbar. To use one that is not visible, click the down-facing arrow at the end of a toolbar and click **Add or Remove Buttons** to find the missing button (see Figure 1.2).

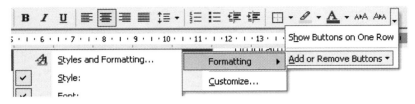

Figure 1.2

You will see a bar down the right-hand side of the screen which is known as the Task Pane. It offers shortcuts to various actions, but it can be removed to give you more room. Either click the **Close** button in the top corner:

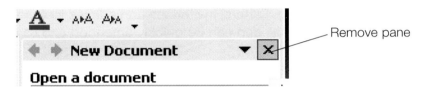

Remove pane

Figure 1.3

or open the **View** menu, wait for it to expand fully (or click the double arrows at the bottom to offer all the options) and then click **Task Pane** to take off the tick and remove it from your screen.

Figure 1.4

The flashing black bar on your page – the cursor – shows the position for your text. There is always a margin round the page so that the document will print correctly, and a temporary name for your work (*Document 1*) will show in the Title bar (see Figure 1.5).

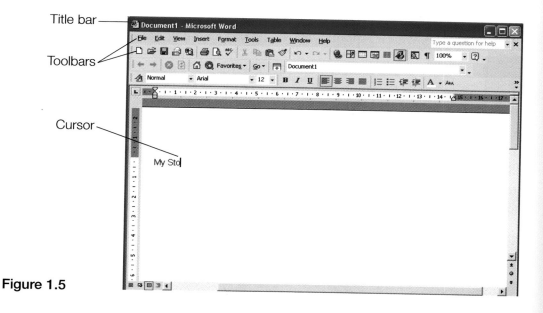

Figure 1.5

If you carry out very little word processing, it's a good idea to get to know some of the special keys on the keyboard before you start:

Figure 1.6

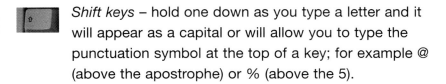

Shift keys – hold one down as you type a letter and it will appear as a capital or will allow you to type the punctuation symbol at the top of a key; for example @ (above the apostrophe) or % (above the 5).

Control keys – hold one down as you press a letter key to act as a shortcut to common actions; for example with S – save, with P – print, with N – new document, etc.

Enter – press to move the text insertion point down a line, or to OK an action.

Arrow keys – press to move the cursor in that direction.

Backspace – erase text to the left of the cursor.

Delete – erase text to the right of the cursor.

Tab key – found to the left of the letter Q – will move the cursor across the page in short jumps.

Word wrap

After typing some text, such as a title for your work, press the Enter key on the keyboard to move the cursor onto the next line, and press it again if you want to leave a blank line before typing the first paragraph.

You do *not* need to press Enter each time you reach the end of a line within a sentence or paragraph as the computer will automatically move the next word onto a new line for you. This process is known as 'word wrap'.

Correcting mistakes

If you notice that you have made a typing error, move the cursor to the word by clicking the mouse pointer on screen. You can also move the cursor into position by pressing an arrow key in the appropriate direction.

Type new letters, or erase a letter or space that you don't want. Erase to the *left* of the cursor by pressing the Backspace key and to the *right* by pressing the Delete key.

We all make silly mistakes, and if you suddenly see that you've typed the same letter several times, or deleted a chunk of your work, click the Undo button 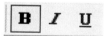 . This will step back through your actions – as long as you haven't saved the changes in the meantime.

Changing the appearance

To make parts of your work stand out, you can change the appearance of your text by the process known as formatting. To type letters **in bold type** first click on the **B** toolbar button. You can <u>underline text</u> by clicking the <u>U</u> button, or change to *italic* typing by clicking the *I* button. Click any of these toolbar buttons again when you are ready to turn *off* the formatting before continuing. You will know when they are on as they will display a blue square (see Figure 1.7).

Figure 1.7

There are different types of character (font) you can choose from, and a list is available if you click the down-facing arrow in the Font box. You can also increase letter size by selecting an alternative number from the Font size box.

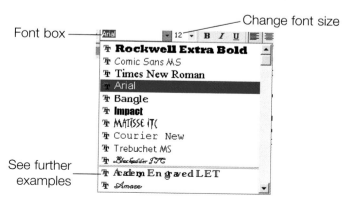

Figure 1.8

Selecting text

If you decide to format your text after it has been typed, select the target text first. Then any formatting will only apply to these words. They will appear as white letters on a black background, and you can click an empty part of the screen to take off the selection again.

This is selected text

This is unselected text

There are a number of ways to select text:

- Double-click a word with the mouse pointer.
- Select a line of text by clicking the pointer in the left-hand margin when it shows a right-facing arrow.
- Click and hold down the left mouse button, then drag the pointer across the words or lines.
- If handling the mouse is difficult, click in front of a word and then hold Shift as you press an arrow key to select along the word or text in your chosen direction.
- Select the whole document by opening the **Edit** menu and clicking **Select All** (a shortcut is to hold down the Ctrl key and press the letter A).

Saving

After typing part of your text, it's a good idea to save it. Any work created on a computer is known as a 'file', although files produced using different applications have common names – for example, word-processed files are called 'documents'.

Click the Save button 💾 to save your document for the first time. This opens the **Save As** box (see Figure 1.9).

You will find that your first text entry has been selected automatically as the name for your work. This is the name you will see when searching for your work in the future. If this is not what you want the file to be named, change it by clicking in the **File name:** box and typing your preferred text instead.

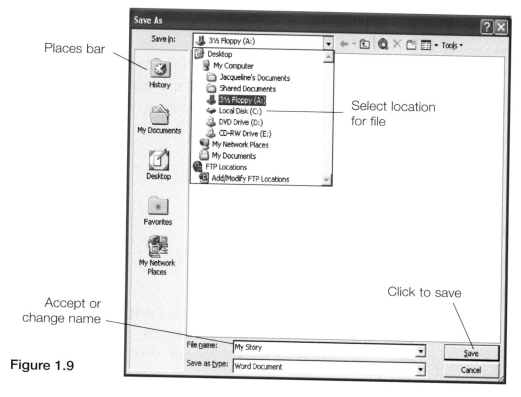

Places bar

Select location
for file

Accept or
change name

Click to save

Figure 1.9

You will also be offered the My Documents folder as the location
for the file. If you want to save it elsewhere – for example onto a
floppy disk – click the drop-down arrow in the **Save in:** box and
select an alternative location, or click one of the folders in the
left-hand Places Bar (see Figure 1.9). Then click **Save**. You will
return to your work and will see that the new file name now
appears in the blue Title bar.

Updating or Save As

To update your work, taking extra typing or amendments into
account and overwriting the original, simply click the **Save** button.

If you want to keep a new version of the document, you need to
save it with a new name or in a different location, so that the
original is not overwritten. To do this, you must open the **Save
As** box, by going to **File – Save As** and changing the file name
and/or location before clicking **Save**.

Closing

Having saved your work, close it at any time by clicking the **Close** button in the top right-hand corner. The red **Close** button will exit Word and you will return to the Desktop, but the lower button will only close your current document (see Figure 1.10).

Exit Word ———   ✕ ——— Close document

Figure 1.10

Printing

To print one copy of your current document, click the **Print** toolbar button. You may prefer to click the **Print Preview** button first, to check how your document will appear when printed (see Figure 1.11).

Print ——— 🖨 🔍 ——— Print Preview

Figure 1.11

Click the button labelled **Close** on the Print Preview toolbar  to return to the document and make any necessary amendments before printing.

To print several copies of your document, or selected pages only, you will need to open the Print dialog box, so go to **File – Print** and set the various options before clicking **OK** (see Figure 1.12).

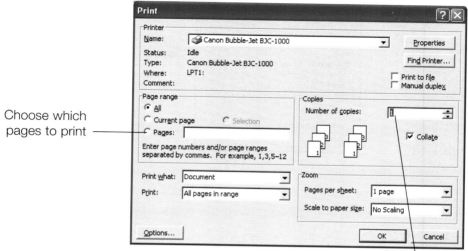

Choose which
pages to print

Figure 1.12

Choose how many copies to print

Project 1

Create a word-processed short story and submit it for publication

One activity that many of us enjoy at any age is writing stories. Magazines pay £100 to £300 for short stories – particularly those with a twist in the tale – and it can be an enjoyable and lucrative hobby. So here are the steps to follow if you want your short story ready for submission to the editor of your favourite magazine.

1. If you follow the advice at the beginning of this chapter, you can type your story as a first draft and save it with a suitable name. Most editors want a story of a certain length, so let your word-processing application count the number of words for you. Just open the **Tools** menu and click **Word Count**. You will see the number of words, pages and even paragraphs, characters and lines (see Figure 1.13). A 1,500 word story takes up about four sides of A4.

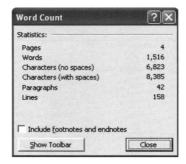

Figure 1.13

2. Editors like to be able to read your story easily, so it is usual to submit it in double line spacing, with blank lines between each line of text.

Single line spacing

Double line spacing

Figure 1.14

A quick way to double line space is to select the text and then hold Ctrl and press the number 2 key. Return to single line spacing with Ctrl plus 1, or 1.5 spacing with Ctrl plus 5.
You can also use the **Line Spacing** toolbar button (see Figure 1.15).

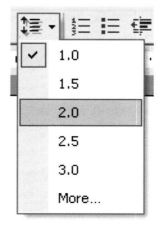

Figure 1.15

3. As you type, you may see red or green lines appearing below some of your words. Red means the word is not listed in the built-in dictionary, and green means that the text is not obeying a common rule of grammar. Green lines will appear, for example, if you leave too few or too many spaces after a comma or full stop. To amend a spelling, *right*-click the red line to display the menu and select an alternative from the list. For a word that is spelt correctly, such as your name, click **Add to Dictionary** so that it is accepted in future, or **Ignore All** to cancel the error message.

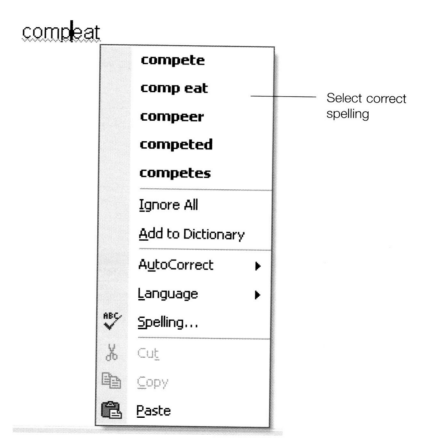

Select correct
spelling

Figure 1.16

Don't forget that the computer will *not* proof-read, so the following sentence will not show any error messages:
He worked a cross to the stares and sit dawn on the bottom steppe.

4. With a story extending across many pages, you will want to make sure that the pages are clearly labelled, for example with your name or title of the story and the date, and that there are page numbers on every page. If you add these as a header or footer – repeated entries that appear in the top or bottom margins – they won't affect the page layouts.

   a. Open the **View – Header and Footer** menu and type an entry, such as the story title, in the box that appears. Move across the box by pressing the tab key to add further details, and apply formats in the normal way.

   b. Select entries such as the date or page numbers from the toolbar. They will appear against a grey background and will be updated automatically as you continue to work on your document.

   c. Add text at the bottom of the page by clicking the **Switch Between** button and entering more details here (see Figure 1.17).

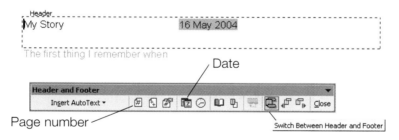

Figure 1.17

   d. When all entries have been completed, either click the **Close** button on the toolbar or double-click the page text (which will appear grey) to return to the document.

   e. To remove entries, double-click the header or footer text to open the box, select the entry and press the Delete key.

5. Long documents can look neater if the right-hand edge is straight. This involves 'justifying' the text. For your front page, or in an accompanying letter, you may want your story title in the centre and your name and address on the right. To reposition any block of text, select it and click the appropriate

alignment button on the toolbar (see Figure 1.18).

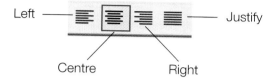

Left — Justify

Figure 1.18

Centre   Right

Note that alignment applies to a whole line. After centring a title, for example, press Enter and click the left alignment button if you want the text on the next line to begin at the left margin.

6. Sometimes, you have a change of heart after typing a story. Perhaps your heroine's name doesn't feel right, but it has appeared several times on every page. To change all the entries quickly, use Word's Replace tool.

   a. Open the **Edit** menu and select **Replace**.

   b. Type the original name in the **Find what:** box and the new name in the **Replace with:** box. If it is straightforward, click **Replace All** and the job is done.

Figure 1.19

Find and Replace	? X

Find   Replace   Go To

Find what: Hermione

Replace with: Henrietta

More ∓   Replace   Replace All   Find Next   Cancel

   c. For words where there may be some confusion, or if you want to leave the original in place in your title or on some of your pages, click **Find Next** and check the entry by eye. To replace it, click **Replace**, but to leave it in place and move to the next entry, click **Find Next** again.

7. On a final read-through of your work, you may decide that some sections are in the wrong place. Instead of typing them

all out again, you can remove them from the document and store them safely in a part of the computer's memory known as the Office Clipboard. They will stay here until you are ready to 'paste' them into their new position, as long as you don't turn off the computer in the meantime.

The process of moving text is known as Cut and Paste. You can carry out Cut and Paste in four steps:

a. Select the text to be moved.

It was a very hot day. I decided not to go out.

b. Click the **Cut** toolbar button ✂ . The words will disappear. (If you want to copy text to a different position but leave the original in place, you click the **Copy** button 📋 instead.)

c. Decide on the new position for the text and click to place the cursor on screen.

I decided not to go out. |

d. Click the **Paste** button 📋 . The text will appear.

e. (This step is optional and you can ignore the button, but you could decide whether to apply a new format or retain the original by selecting an option offered by clicking the **Paste Options** button 📋 ▾ .)

8. Having printed your story, type an accompanying letter and then send it off. To learn how to add the address to an envelope, see Chapter 2.

Project 2

Create folders to store your work

As you write more and more stories and use your computer for letters and other documents, you will find that your original storage folder becomes too full for you to find individual pieces of work again easily. It may therefore be a good idea to start a file storage system. You can do this within the My Documents folder or, if you use removable disks, on one of these. Eventually, you will build up a large hierarchy of folders that will be much quicker to search.

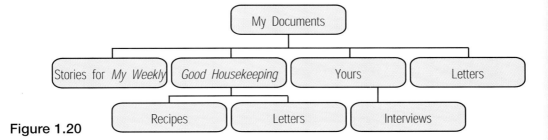

Figure 1.20

1. Open My Computer on the Desktop and click the link to My Documents in the Task Pane or a Floppy disk in the A: drive.

Open top level folder

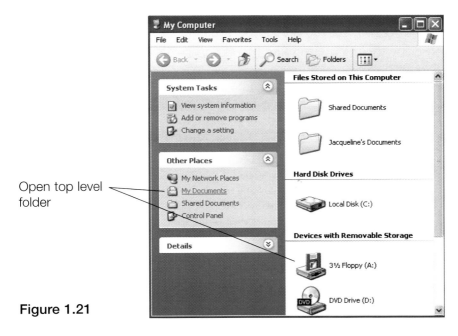

Figure 1.21

2. You will see all the documents you have created and saved so far. These can be viewed and reorganised in a number of ways. You can display large or small icons, a list or thumbnails of any pictures. Files can also be organised alphabetically by name or by date created. Change the display by clicking the appropriate option on the **View** menu or **Views** button, and change the order by selecting **Arrange Icons by**.

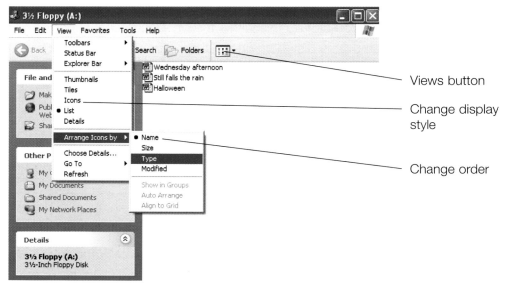

Figure 1.22

3. Having decided how you want to group your files, for example by publication or by topic, click the **File** menu and select **New – Folder** (see Figure 1.23).

Figure 1.23

4. An empty folder will appear within the window and you can type its name over the blue text. (Folders are shown as yellow boxes, whereas files display the icon for the program used to create them.)

File icon

Folder icon

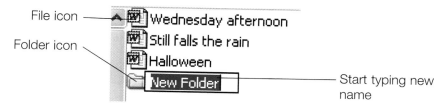

Start typing new name

Figure 1.24

5. To move any of the files visible in the window into the folder, simply click and drag them towards the folder. When it turns blue, let go and the file will be placed inside.

File dragged into folder

Figure 1.25

6. To find a file you have stored inside a folder, you need to open the folder by double-clicking. The stored file will be visible inside.

Reurn to parent folder

New folder

File stored in folder

Figure 1.26

7. An alternative method for working with folders is to click the **Folders** button. This reveals all your folders in the left pane and the contents of any selected folder in the right pane. Any folder showing a + symbol will contain further folders, so click the symbol to open up the folders structure. It will show a – symbol

when fully opened. Move files into folders by dragging them across the division between the two.

Reveal folders on your computer

Flie dragged onto floppy disk

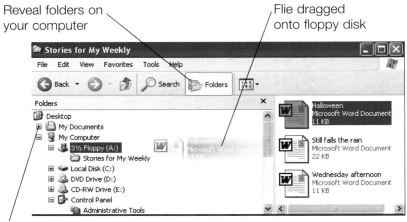

Click to display folders inside

Figure 1.27

8. You can also create folders as you work. Having opened the **Save As** window, click the button to create a new folder when the appropriate parent folder is showing in the **Save in:** window. You can now save your work directly into this new folder.

Create new folder

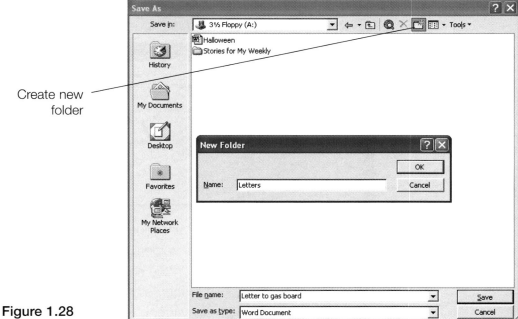

Figure 1.28

Project 3

Design an advertisement for a local newspaper

Having mastered the basics of Word, it can be fun to explore the display features. These include setting the text in columns, adding pictures and applying attractive borders. Here is how you could go about designing an advertisement for an unwanted fish tank. You will need the Drawing toolbar – if it is not showing along the bottom of the screen, *right*-click any toolbar and select it from the list.

1. After drafting out the advertisement on paper, you may decide you want it to include main text and then a description in two short columns. Type the text normally first of all and then select the description.

Aquarium for sale

4ft mahogany cabinet, very good condition complete with filter, heater and magnetic glass cleaner. Fish include 3 guppies and 6 platys, together with several shrimps. Also includes a number of small snails that are useful for keeping the tank clean. Fresh weed included, as well as a bag of gravel and 2 plastic plants.

Figure 1.29

£75 only cash accepted. Tel: 01444 677893

2. Open the **Format** menu and select **Columns**. In the dialog box, select the two-column option and add a tick in the box if you would like to include a vertical line. Then click **OK**.

Two columns

Include line between

Figure 1.30a

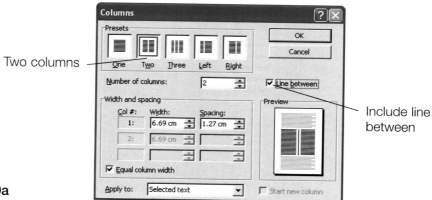

Aquarium for Sale
4ft mahogany cabinet, very good
condition complete with filter,
heater and magnetic glass cleaner.
Fish include 3 guppies and 6
platys, together with several

shrimps. Also includes a number
of small snails that are useful for
keeping the tank clean. Fresh
weed included, as well as a bag of
gravel and 2 plastic plants

Figure 1.30b
£75 only cash accepted. Tel:014444 677893

3. If the text isn't distributed evenly between the columns when you return to the page, click in front of the first word that you want at the start of the *second* column, open the **Insert** menu and click **Break**. Select the **Column break** option and then **OK**.

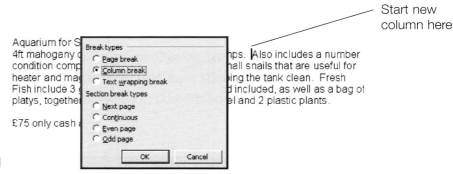

Start new
column here

Figure 1.31

4. You can apply different formats to the title, description and contact details, so that the advertisement looks more attractive. You can also centre the title and any other text as necessary and then add a border. For example, select the title, go to **Format – Borders and Shading** and apply a simple or shadowed box with double line style. For a coloured background you could also click the **Shading** tab and select a colour from the palette.

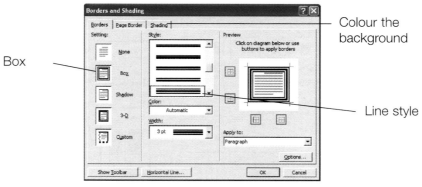

Colour the
background

Box

Line style

Figure 1.32a

> **Aquarium for Sale**
>
> | 4ft mahogany cabinet, very good condition complete with filter, heater and magnetic glass cleaner. Fish include 3 guppies and 6 platys, together with several shrimps. | Also includes a number of small snails that are useful for keeping the tank clean. Fresh weed included, as well as a bag of gravel and 2 plastic plants |
> | --- | --- |
>
> £75 only cash accepted. Tel:014444 677893

Figure 1.32b

5. Finally, make the advertisement stand out by adding a picture of a fish. There are two options if you don't take your own photographs: use an image included in Word's Clip Art Gallery, or find a picture on the World Wide Web.

   a. *Clip Art:* Click the **Insert Clip Art** toolbar button on the Draw toolbar at the bottom of the screen to open the search pane on the right of your page (see Figure 1.33).

Figure 1.33

Figure 1.34

Type in your subject and click **Search**. When the results appear, scroll down to find one you like. To repeat the search with new search words, click **Modify** (see Figure 1.34). Click a picture you like to add it to the page. (As many of the pictures will not have been installed on your computer, make sure that your Microsoft Office XP Content CD-ROM is available.)

When the picture appears, it may be in the wrong place and the wrong size. To reduce its size, click to reveal the border and move the pointer over a corner box (known as a sizing handle). Drag this inwards when the pointer displays a two-way arrow (see Figure 1.35).

Figure 1.35

Drag inwards

To move the whole picture into position on the page, open the **Draw** menu on the toolbar and select **Text Wrapping – Tight**.

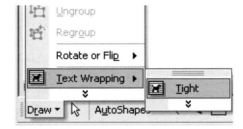

Figure 1.36

This will change the black sizing handles on the border to white circles, and you will now be able to drag the picture with your mouse. Readjust the text so that the finished advertisement is as you want it.

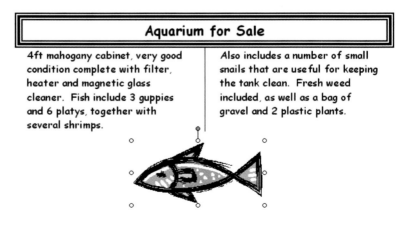

Aquarium for Sale

4ft mahogany cabinet, very good condition complete with filter, heater and magnetic glass cleaner. Fish include 3 guppies and 6 platys, together with several shrimps.

Also includes a number of small snails that are useful for keeping the tank clean. Fresh weed included, as well as a bag of gravel and 2 plastic plants.

£75 only cash accepted. Tel:014444 677893

Figure 1.37

b. *Web image*: If you prefer to find a picture on the World Wide Web, and know how to search (see Chapter 8), use a search engine to look for images. Adding *clipart* in the search box should help ensure that the pictures are free of copyright, but you need to check this before your advertisement is published in a newspaper.

Right-click an image and select **Copy**, and then return to your advertisement and click **Paste**.

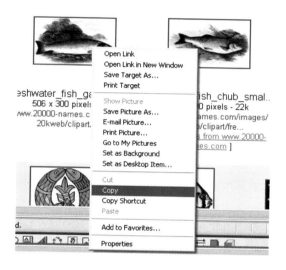

Figure 1.38

You can now carry out the editing, as explained above, to position this picture on your page instead.

Aquarium for Sale

4ft mahogany cabinet, very good condition complete with filter, heater and magnetic glass cleaner. Fish include 3 guppies and 6 platys, together with several shrimps.

Also includes a number of small snails that are useful for keeping the tank clean. Fresh weed included, as well as a bag of gravel and 2 plastic plants.

£75 only cash accepted. Tel:014444 677893

Figure 1.39

2

Envelopes and labels

Word makes printing envelopes and labels very easy and efficient. You can print the same label on a sheet of label paper, or create differently-worded labels as well as individually addressed envelopes.

Having typed a letter that includes the address of the recipient, it is a good idea to use this straightaway to print out an envelope. Simply select the full address and click **Tools – Letters and Mailings – Envelopes and Labels**. Click the **Envelopes** tab and the address will show in the window. You can make changes to it if you need to by clicking in the box.

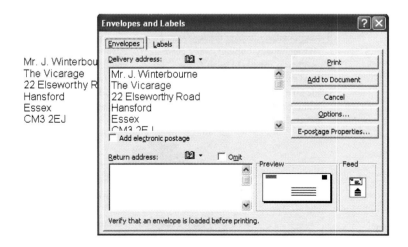

Mr. J. Winterbou
The Vicarage
22 Elseworthy R
Hansford
Essex
CM3 2EJ

Figure 2.1

For unusually sized envelopes, click **Options** and pick a size. Then click the **Printing Options** tab to set the position for the envelope to be fed into your printer (see Figure 2.2).

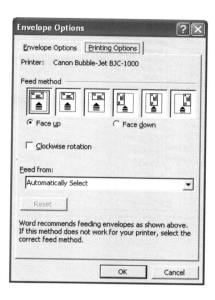

Figure 2.2

Back in the Envelopes window, click **Add to Document** if you want to keep both envelope and letter together to print later, or click **Print** and print your envelope directly.

Project 4

Print out a set of labels

1. To produce a set of different labels, open the **Envelopes and Labels** window as above, but then click the **Labels** tab.
2. The first task is to select appropriate label sizes by clicking **Options**. If you have purchased special sticky-backed label paper, the pack will show the sizes. Some manufacturers' labels will be listed in the computer window and you can select the company and then find the exact size or code. For unusual sizes, you will need to click the **New Label** button and set the correct measurements yourself.

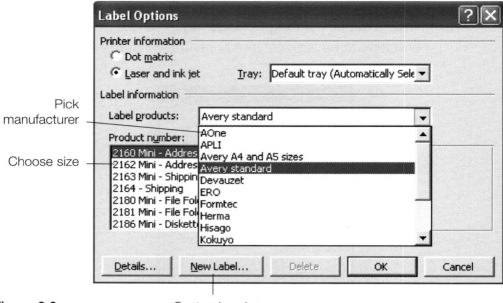

Pick manufacturer

Choose size

Figure 2.3   Customise size

3. Click **OK** and make sure that you check in the main window that you will be producing a sheet of labels, rather than one label in the centre of the page (see Figure 2.4).

Figure 2.4

4. Now click **New Document** and you will see a grid of empty labels on the page. Click in each one and type the name and address – you will only have a few text lines available. Press Enter to move onto a new line.

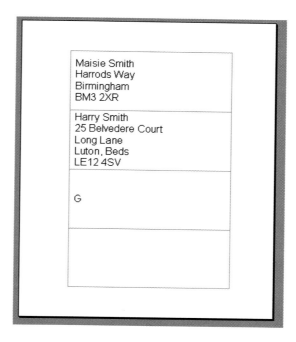

Figure 2.5

5. Having typed all the labels, either print straightaway or save the document to print another time.

6. To produce a full page of the *same* label, type the details in the **Envelopes and Labels** window before printing or clicking **New Document**.

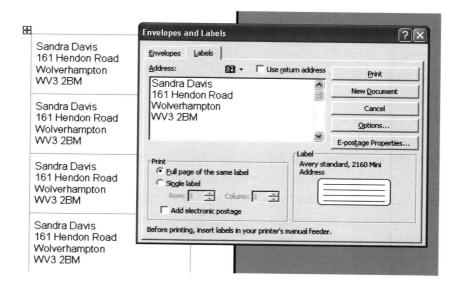

Figure 2.6

3

Digital cameras

Once you have used a digital camera, you will find it very hard to return to a conventional one. Not only can you see small 'thumbnails' of your pictures as soon as they are taken, you need never buy film again. Simply save the pictures you want to keep onto your computer, discard the rest and use the camera over and over again.

Once the pictures are on your computer, you can use image-editing software to change any parts you don't like, and the improved pictures can then be stored on disk, sent via email to relatives and friends, or printed out. Using good-quality photographic paper will allow you to produce prints as good as those that, in the past, you might have collected from Boots or Bonusprint.

Resolution

The major consideration when using a digital camera is its resolution. This is the measure of how much detail shows in a picture (ie the sharpness of the image), and relates to the number of dots of colour (pixels) per inch (ppi). As the pixel number is fixed, the more you enlarge a picture, the less clear it will become until, like newsprint, you will start to see each dot that makes up the image. It is therefore important to consider how sharp you want your picture to be when it is printed at a particular size. For most purposes, you should try to print your picture at a resolution of 300 ppi.

When it comes to buying a digital camera, you will find them described as having a resolution of between 2 and 5 megapixels. A mid-range digital camera with a resolution of 3 megapixels will produce images containing 2,000 × 1,500 pixels, and will print out good quality pictures 7" × 5" (18 cm × 12.5 cm) and satisfactory pictures 8" × 6" (20 cm × 15 cm) in size.

A balance has to be struck between how sharp you want your final images to be and the size of the image file, because large, high resolution images are slower to work with and take up more room on your computer.

Software

Before you can see the pictures on your computer, you need to insert the CD-ROM and follow the instructions to install software, such as FinePixViewer for example, that will have come with your camera. You may prefer to install more advanced image-editing software, such as Paint Shop Pro or PhotoShop, which will enable you both to work with your camera images and carry out more sophisticated editing. You can find out more about using one of these programs in Project 9 on page 60.

Project 5

Take a picture of your pet, store it on your computer and print out a copy

It is important to read the manual and get to know your own digital camera settings before starting this project.

1. Your camera should be ready to use straightaway, as all it requires is a battery and the Image Memory Card that enables you to record the digital images electronically and store them until you are ready to transfer them onto a computer. Turn on the camera, make sure that the dial is set to still photography

(usually showing a coloured camera symbol: see Figure 3.1) and then aim, focus and release the shutter exactly as you would when using a conventional camera to take pictures.

Figure 3.1

2. Take a few pictures of your pet from different angles, or use the zoom, and then, if you want to, preview them on the camera. Change the dial to playback mode (usually showing a solid arrow symbol) and press the forward and backward arrows on the camera to move through the images. At this point, if you want to take more pictures and you have not bought an extra large Memory Card, you could erase unwanted images by clicking the menu button and clicking the delete option.

3. When you have finished taking pictures of your pet and want to view them properly, you need to connect the camera to your computer. Turn off the camera, but you can leave the computer switched on. Plug one end of the cable into the camera and the other into a spare USB slot (a free point for connecting extra hardware items) at the back, or sometimes the front, of your computer.

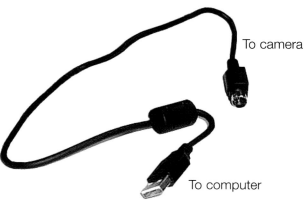

To camera

To computer

Figure 3.2

4. Turn on the camera, and your software may start up automatically. If not, find it from an icon on the Desktop or the **Start – All Programs** menu and click the appropriate folder in the left-hand list. All the pictures on the camera will be displayed as small, medium or large 'thumbnails'. In the folders list, the camera will show as a separate drive alongside the floppy disk and CD-ROM drives – perhaps named something like 'Removable Disk' – and you may need to open one or more subfolders to locate your images.

Find camera and folder containing the pictures

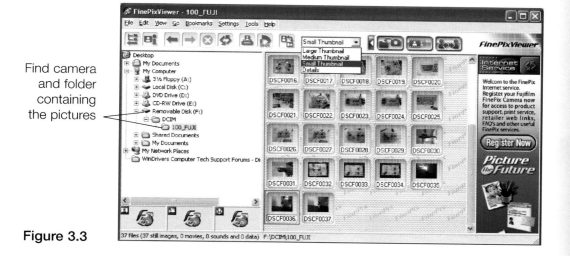

Figure 3.3

5. One option when viewing pictures is to click the **Slide Show** toolbar button (see Figure 3.4) and watch them that way. The toolbars and menus will disappear, and you will see each picture in full-screen mode. Wait as the next picture is revealed, or click the mouse to exit or delete a particular image.

Figure 3.4

6. Double-click any thumbnail image to open it fully. You can now carry out some basic editing using the toolbar provided (see Figure 3.5).

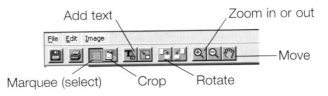

Add text

Zoom in or out

Move

Figure 3.5

Marquee (select)

Crop

Rotate

Most types of software have similar tools. For example, you can cut off unwanted parts by clicking on the **Marquee** (select) button, drawing round the area of the picture you want to keep and then clicking the **Crop** button (see Figure 3.6).

Select area to keep

Cropped picture

Figure 3.6

Rotate your image left or right by clicking the appropriate **Rotate** button, and add text by clicking on the **Text** button and then typing in the box that will appear. After clicking **OK**, move the text to an appropriate position with your pointer.

7. For images you want to keep, click the **Save** button or go to **File – Save As** and make sure that you change any numbered file name to one that is more memorable.

Figure 3.7

8. You may be directed to save images in a folder labelled My Pictures, within the My Documents folder automatically set aside for saving all your work, but you can always choose an alternative location if you prefer. Click the arrow in the **Save in**: box and select a different drive, or open a folder showing in the **Save As** window.

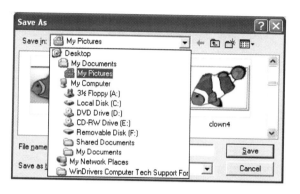

Figure 3.8

9. If you want to open your pictures directly into an image-editing program, open the program, click **File – Browse** and open the camera folder to view thumbnails of the images. Double-click any picture to view, save or start making changes.

10. To print a good quality picture, you will need to buy photographic paper from a high street stationer or via the Internet. You can even buy packs of photo greetings cards that have a glossy coating and can be folded. They will come with appropriately sized envelopes and may also include software that helps you position your picture correctly on the page (see Project 7 about greetings cards on page 44).

11. Open the picture and go to **File – Print** or click the **Print** toolbar button to display the printer settings dialog box. Click **Properties** and select the correct paper and colour settings before clicking **OK**.

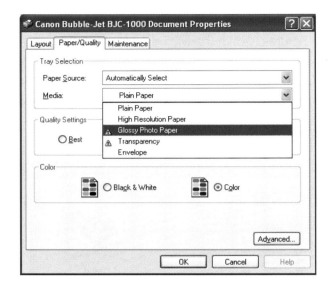

Figure 3.9

12. Sometimes you may want to print several images on a single piece of paper or produce different size prints. If you open your pictures using Windows Picture and Fax Viewer (select by right-clicking and choosing **Open with…**), you can click the **Printer** icon and then use the **Photo Printing Wizard** to take you through the set-up.

Click for Wizard

Figure 3.10

13. Select **Contact Sheet Prints** for this option, or choose from a range of printing sizes.

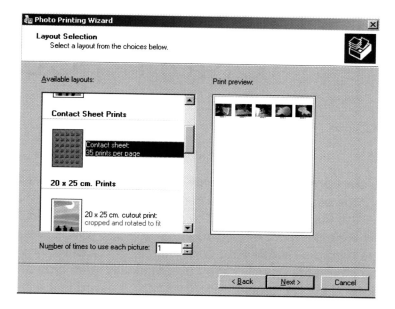

Figure 3.11

4

Creating CDs

As you start producing documents, use your digital camera to take photos or visit Websites to find information or music that you want to keep, you will need to save copies of your files somewhere safe. Most of the programs you use will be saved onto the hard disk inside your computer, in the C: drive. Any files that you create are usually saved automatically in an area of the disk labelled My Documents. Pictures will be saved in a sub-folder labelled My Pictures, and as you saw in Project 2, you can create a range of different folders if you want to group certain types of file together.

Soon, you will find that you need extra storage space – perhaps for files you aren't sure you want to keep but are not ready to delete, or for backup copies of important files in case your computer crashes and you lose the originals.

Sometimes you may only want to keep small files, or need to take files with you to another computer, and it is therefore easiest to save them onto a floppy disk. Each disk can hold up to 1.44 Mb and in the machine is referred to as 3½ inch Floppy (A:) drive. This is because the disk is read from the A: drive which is a slot at the front of your computer.

Modern computers also have drives that can read multimedia CD-ROMs and music CDs or DVDs, and as CDs can store over 450 times the amount of data as a floppy disk, many people now create their own disks as a form of extra storage. Some computers have a built-in CD-Writer. If yours does not, you will need to buy one that can be attached externally. These writers work by using a laser to 'burn' files onto the CD.

The software needed to create the disks is already installed on Windows XP machines, but for other operating systems there are a range of programs that you can buy including Nero, Roxio Easy CD Creator and Pinnacle Instant CD.

CD-R or CD-RW?

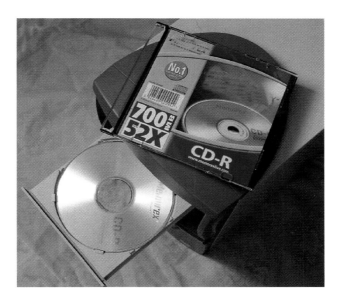

Figure 4.1

There are two main types of disk that can be used in CD-Writers:

CD-R stands for CD-Recordable and these disks can only be written to once. When they are full, you cannot erase or write over the files. However, they are usually quite cheap to buy and can be read by most CD–ROM drives and audio CD players.

CD-RW stands for CD-Rewritable as these disks allow you to amend files and rewrite to them many times. They cannot always be read by standard CD-ROM drives and are much more expensive than CD-Rs and so are best used when you want to work regularly on your files. Once you have enough material and won't want to make any more changes, transfer the files to CD-Rs for long-term storage.

Project 6

Store backup copies of your pictures on a CD

1. Place a new CD-R or CD-RW in the CD drive and wait for the dialog box to open on screen. The selected option will be to view the contents of the disk, so click **OK** (see Figure 4.2).

Figure 4.2

2. For a new disk, nothing will show. You now need to locate the files you want to copy. Click the Up arrow or link to My Documents and browse through your files to locate your pictures (see Figure 4.3).

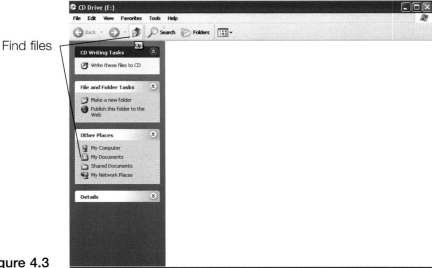

Figure 4.3

3. When you reach the appropriate folder, such as My Pictures, select a picture by clicking it with the mouse. You can select several pictures by holding down the Ctrl key as you click each one. When all the pictures you want to save onto the CD have been selected, click the menu option **Copy the selected items** in the Picture Tasks Pane (see Figure 4.4).

Click to copy ——

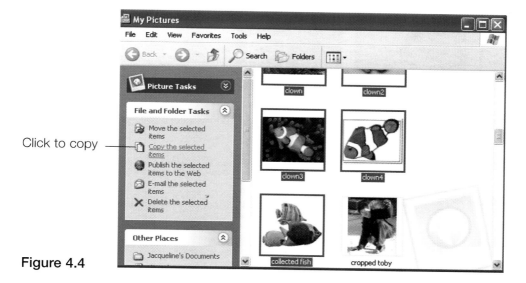

Figure 4.4

4. Find the CD Drive in the list and click **Copy**.

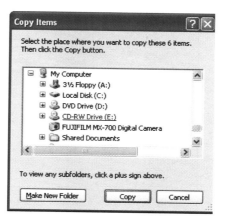

Figure 4.5

5. You will return to the CD Drive window and your files will be displayed ready for writing to the CD.

6. Select the option **Write these files to CD** and, if you want to, name the disk when asked to do so.

Start writing process

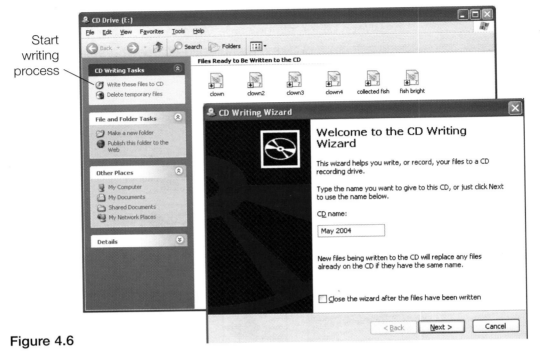

Figure 4.6

7. Click **Next** and the files will start to be copied.

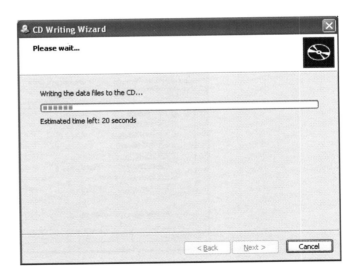

Figure 4.7

8. At the end of the writing process, your disk will be ejected from the drive so that you can label it and put it away for safe keeping.

Greetings cards with PowerPoint

Cards can be expensive, so having a computer allows you to make your own personalised cards extremely cheaply. If you do not have a digital camera or scanner and want to use someone else's pictures, you have two choices: use the Clip Art available with Microsoft Office applications (see Project 3 on page 19); or find a picture on the Web (searching the Web is explained in Project 10 on page 71).

If you want to find a picture on the Web, type the subject of your picture into the search box at any search engine Website, and, if available, select an image-only search.

Search for
pictures only

Figure 5.1

If you include the word *clipart* in the search box, you should find images free of copyright that you can use in your cards. Click a small image to see further details and, when it opens, click the link to see it full size.

Click to view full size —

Can be used —

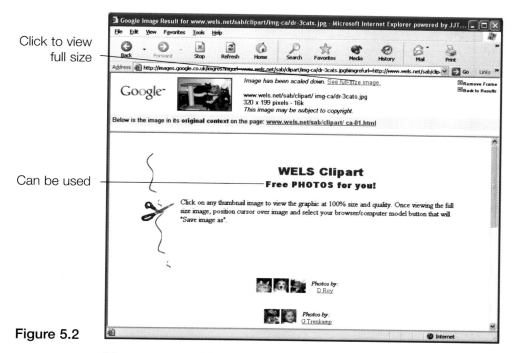

Figure 5.2

You can now either copy it straight from the Website into your card, or save it onto your computer to insert later. To save the picture, *right*-click the image and select **Save Picture As**. The **Save As** window will open and you can name and save the file as normal. If you choose **Copy**, make your card as explained below and, at any stage, *right*-click the slide and select **Paste** to add the picture.

Save to computer

Copy into memory and paste directly into the card —

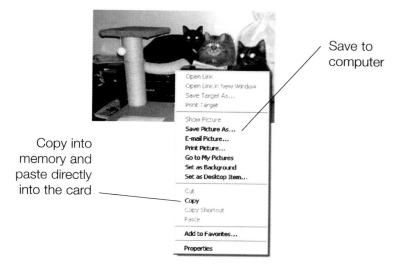

Figure 5.3

Project 7

Create a birthday card using a picture you have taken

1. Although a desktop publication package such as Publisher makes card-making very easy, many people do not buy this extra program. Within the basic Office XP suite, the presentation software PowerPoint can be used instead. You will need to set out the card like this:

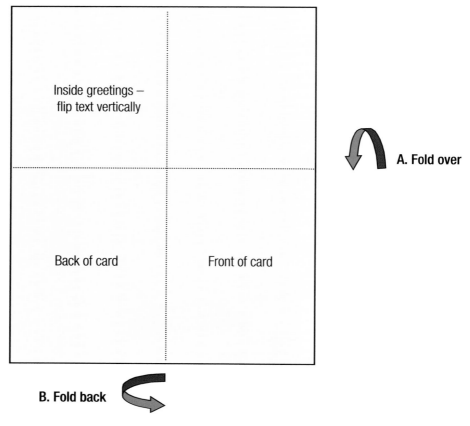

Inside greetings – flip text vertically

A. Fold over

Back of card

Front of card

B. Fold back

Figure 5.4

2. Open PowerPoint by clicking the icon [icon] or selecting it from the **Start – All Programs** menu, and go to **Format – Slide Layout** (see Figure 5.5). Your 'page' is referred to as a slide.

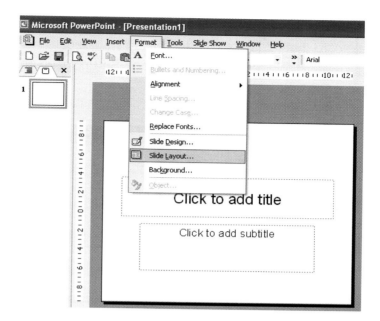

Figure 5.5

3. Select a blank slide from the list and click to apply it to your slide (see Figure 5.6).

Click this option

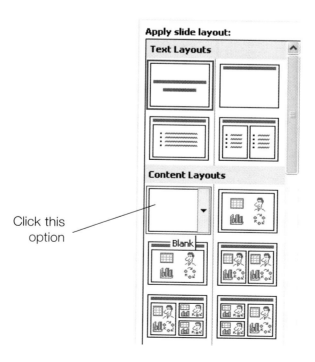

Figure 5.6

4. The slides are in landscape orientation, which will allow you to create a card that folds from the top. If you want a card with a book (sideways) fold, open the **File – Page Setup** menu and change to **Portrait** (see Figure 5.7).

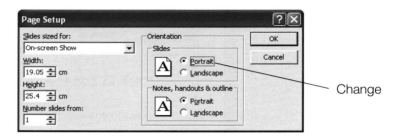

Figure 5.7

5. You are now ready to design the front of the card. To help you work within the relevant sectors of the slide, add non-printing guidelines from the **View – Grid and Guides** menu (see Figure 5.8).

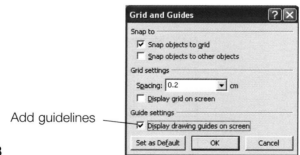

Figure 5.8

6. To include any image saved on your computer, go to **Insert – Picture – From File** or click the **Insert Picture** button 🖼 on the Drawing toolbar and locate your picture. Select it, click **Insert** and it will appear on the slide. It will probably be far too large, so move your mouse over a corner white sizing circle, hold down the left button and drag the boundary inwards when the pointer changes to a two-way arrow. Let go and the picture will be much smaller.

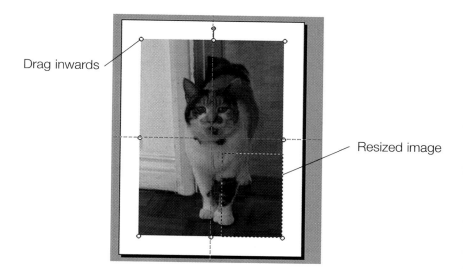

Drag inwards

Resized image

Figure 5.9

7. Continue to adjust the size if necessary and then drag the picture into position when the pointer shows a four-way arrow. (If appropriate, you could also drag the green circle left or right to rotate the image.)

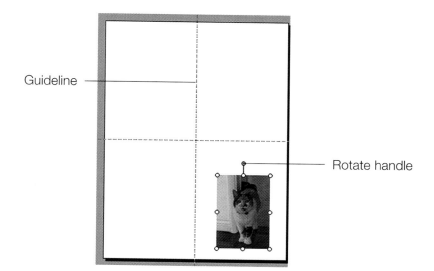

Guideline

Rotate handle

Figure 5.10

8. Now you can add some text to the front of the card. You have two choices: Text Boxes or WordArt objects:
   a. Text Box – Click on the **Text Box** button and drag the mouse across the slide when the pointer shows a cross. This will create

a small box with the cursor inside, and you can start typing straightaway (see Figure 5.11). Note that you will need to increase the text font size in order to fill the space as you cannot simply stretch the box.

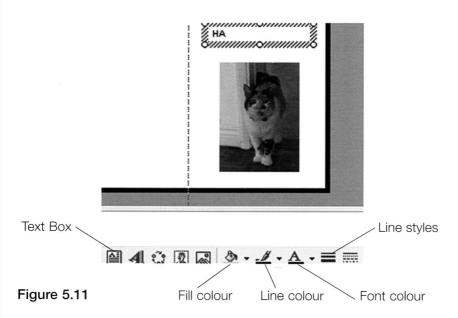

Text Box   Line styles

Figure 5.11   Fill colour   Line colour   Font colour

Colour the letters by selecting from the **Font Colour** drop-down arrow, and add coloured borders or fill to the Text Box from other Drawing toolbar buttons.

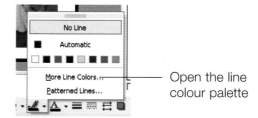

Open the line
colour palette

Figure 5.12

Change the style, size, position and appearance of the text using the formatting toolbar buttons (see Figure 5.13) or **Format – Font** menu options.

Figure 5.13

Finally, adjust the position of the box so that it is centred above your picture, and add a second box underneath if you want more text on the front of the card.

Figure 5.14

Happy Birthday

b. WordArt – Click the **WordArt** button on the Drawing toolbar to add a text object that can be shaped, stretched and coloured. Select your preferred font style from the gallery (see Figure 5.15).

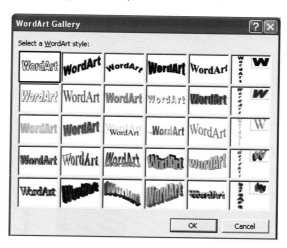

Figure 5.15

Type the text for the card and click **OK** (see Figure 5.16).

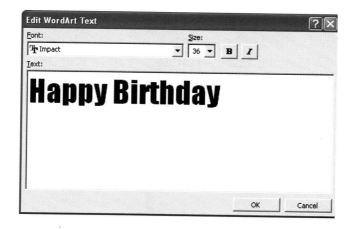

Figure 5.16

Make other changes from the toolbar that will appear
whenever the WordArt is selected (see Figure 5.17).

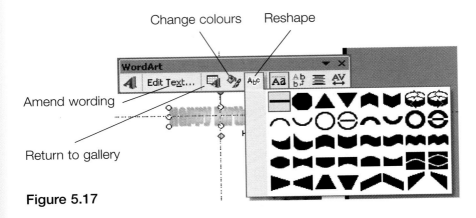

Figure 5.17

Resize and move the WordArt so that it fits the space
above your picture.

Figure 5.18

9. Repeat the addition of WordArt, Text Boxes and pictures for the
    back and inside of the card. However, so that the words can be
    read, you will need to flip any inside text *vertically* by selecting
    this option from the **Draw – Rotate** or **Flip** toolbar menu.

Figure 5.19

10. When the card is complete, print it onto normal paper or specially purchased greetings card or photographic paper. If not straightforward A4 size, make sure that you position the text and pictures appropriately. (Some greetings card packs will even include software to help you position the contents, add text and print correctly.)

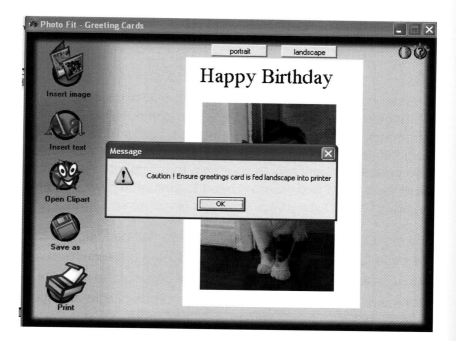

Figure 5.20

6

Scanners

Scanners allow you to capture pictures, text or drawings from the printed page and convert them into computerised information that you can then work with. Scanners vary in price from £40 to over £250, with some of the more expensive models also doubling as printers. If you want to turn printed words into word-processed text, you will need to ensure that your scanner includes OCR (Optical Character Recognition) software.

The most versatile scanners are known as 'flat bed', as you lay the page face down on a glass plate housing the scan head and can scan bulky books by leaving off the cover of the machine. The scan head is made up of an array of hundreds of light-sensitive sensors, together with a light source, mirrors to reflect the image, filters, and a lens. The picture is acquired by the scan head moving slowly across the document on a belt attached to a motor.

As with digital cameras, resolution is important as it relates to the sharpness of the final image. Resolution is determined by the number of sensors within the array. To produce images with a resolution of 300 × 300 dots per inch (dpi), the scanner will have several thousand sensors, but some scanners use software to 'interpolate' extra dots (pixels) between those actually scanned to add perceived detail to the image.

If you buy a new scanner, connect it to your computer and then use the disk provided to install the software that will control the machine and enable you to work with your images.

Project 8

Scan in a painting and add it to a poster

It is important to read the manual and get to know your own scanner settings before starting the project. As scanner menus can look very different, this project uses examples from two different programs – Hewlett Packard Director and Image-In Color.

1. Lay your picture face down on the scanning plate and open the software program. There may be an icon on the Desktop or you will need to find it from the **Start – All Programs** menu.

Figure 6.1

2. Click the button that starts the process; for example **Scan** or **Import – TWAIN – Acquire**. (TWAIN is a standard that allows image-editing programs to acquire images from a range of scanners.) There may be extra options, such as using your scanner as a photocopier.

Click to start ────

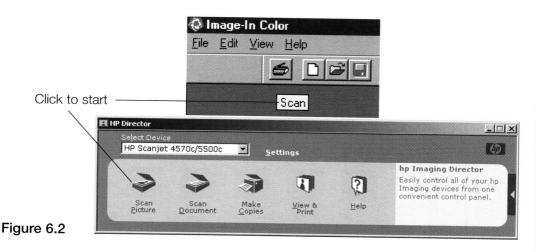

Figure 6.2

3. You may need to click a **Prescan** button, or you may automatically see the image in preview mode. This will allow

you to set up the scanner for your particular image. Reduce the size of the target image by dragging in the boundaries if you don't need the whole page scanned, and select the type of image you want to produce – black and white, greyscale or colour. Use the toolbar buttons, menus or panel settings to amend the contrast and brightness and set an appropriate resolution: text below 300 dpi may look grainy and be hard to read, but coloured images may be quite acceptable at a lower resolution.

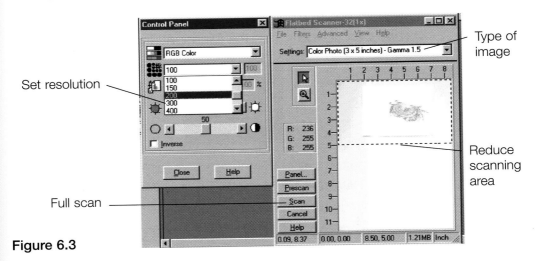

Set resolution

Full scan

Figure 6.3

Type of image

Reduce scanning area

Select scanning area

Open menu to make basic adjustments

Full scan

Figure 6.4

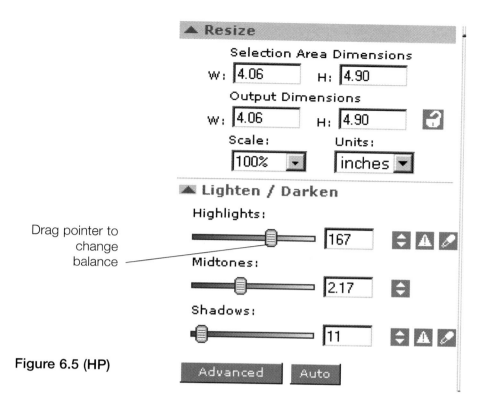

Drag pointer to
change
balance

Figure 6.5 (HP)

4. Click the button to scan your image. The higher the resolution, the slower this process will be.

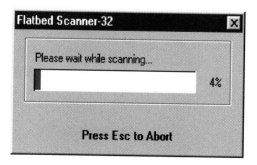

Figure 6.6

5. Eventually, your picture will appear on screen. Depending on your software, you will be able to work on it directly or will need to double-click to open into your editing package. Change the magnification if necessary to view the whole document properly.

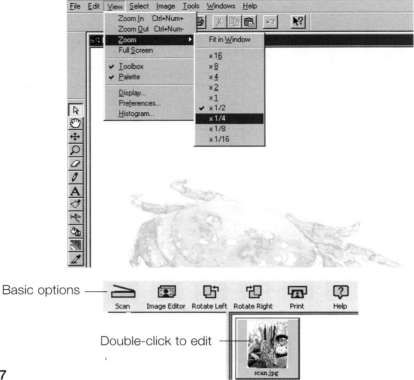

Basic options

Double-click to edit

Figure 6.7

6. Use any of the tools available to make changes. For example, change the colours, add text or select parts with the selection arrow and click **Crop** to remove unwanted areas of the picture.

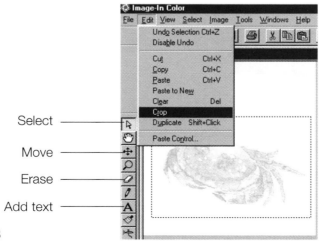

Select

Move

Erase

Add text

Figure 6.8

Adjust settings

Open colour panel

Add text

Figure 6.9 (HP)

7. To keep the image safe, it's a good idea to save it before making any changes. Your system may be set to save scanned images as a particular image file type (such as .tif), but you should be able to choose a compressed format that will save space (such as .jpg files).

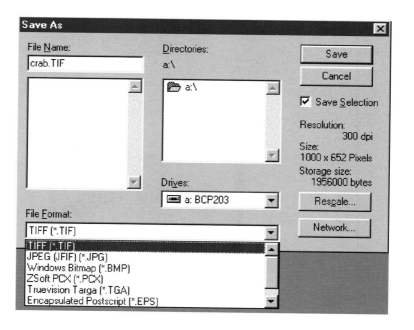

Figure 6.10

8. To copy the scanned picture into a Word document (or other application you may want to work with such as PowerPoint), use the selection tool or menu to select all or part of the image

and then click the **Copy** button. Open your new document (you can minimise or close the scanning software window first), *right*-click on the page and select **Paste**.

9. To produce a poster, it is easiest to use PowerPoint. After your scanned picture has been pasted onto a slide, adjust its size and position (see Project 7 on making a greetings card on page 44). Colour the page by selecting **Format – Background** and choosing a colour from the drop-down list in the box (see Figure 6.11).

Click arrow for colours

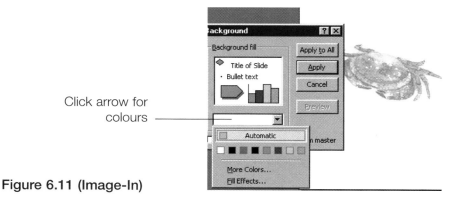

Figure 6.11 (Image-In)

10. Add text in a Text Box or as WordArt and then click the **Print** button to print out a copy of your poster.

Figure 6.12

Improving your photos

Do you have treasured old photographs that are looking a little the worse for wear? Perhaps they are scratched, the colours have faded, or they are even torn in places. Fortunately, you can now combine the use of a scanner and special editing software to make them look nearly as good as new.

You will need to install a dedicated computer program for this activity. Such programs are called graphics or image editors. You can buy cut-down versions or download trial versions and they all work in a similar way. Some commonly available packages include Jasc Paint Shop Pro, Adobe PhotoShop Elements, Serif PhotoPlus, Microsoft Digital Image Pro and Procreate Painter Classic.

There are so many tools and special effects that it can take many weeks to master them all. However, here are some simple effects that you can apply using the automatic settings.

Project 9

Restore an old photo

1. Having installed your software, open it and scan in the photo you have positioned on the glass plate of your scanner. We will use Paint Shop Pro for this project. To begin the process you need to access the scanner by opening the **File** menu and selecting **Import – TWAIN – Acquire**, as the TWAIN technology can acquire images from a range of scanners (see Figure 7.1). When scanning finishes, select **File – End TWAIN session**. (If you find you cannot open your scanner from the image editor, scan the photo as normal, save it and then open the saved image file from the **File – Open** menu.)

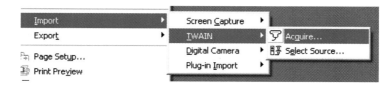

Figure 7.1

2. The image will appear in its own window inside the Paint Shop Pro workspace, and you can save it now, just in case the changes you make need to be repeated or cancelled. Save it in the software's own file type (.psp for Paint Shop Pro) so that you can work on it using all the tools available.

Figure 7.2

3. *Scratch removal:* If there are scratches, or scratched areas, draw round them using one of the selection tools: the square shape ⬚ selects standard areas and the lasso allows you to draw round unusual shapes ⟨lasso icon⟩ . Once selected, a flashing dotted line (a Marquee) shows the selected area.

Figure 7.3

Now open the **Effects** menu, select **Enhance Photo** and click **Automatic Small Scratch Removal**. This will open a dialog box showing 'before' and 'after' images so that you can see the effect of any changes. If your scratch is not camouflaged well enough by the automatic settings, change some of these manually. Preview the whole picture by clicking the **Proof** button (see Figure 7.4). When settings are acceptable, click **OK** and when you are back in the photo, double-click on the screen to remove the Marquee.

Proof button
to preview
picture

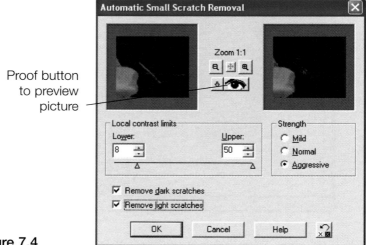

Figure 7.4

4. *Repairing tears*: These normally show as white areas, and the best way to remove them is to 'paint' over them with another part of the image, such as sky or grass. This process, which is known as 'cloning', is equally useful for camouflaging objects in the picture that you don't want, such as the red piece of biscuit on the blanket in our example (see Figure 7.2). The process is carried out in three steps:
   a. Click on the **Cloning** toolbar button .
   b. *Right*-click the pointer over the area you want to use as your camouflage, such as an empty part of the white blanket.
   c. Using the *left* mouse button, gently click and drag the

mouse to paint over the unwanted object or tear marks.
You may have to repeat the selection process several times
to pick up exactly the right colour or texture.

Before 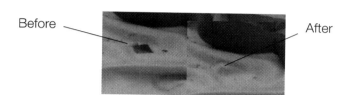 After

Figure 7.5

5. *Colour or contrast enhancement*: If your picture has faded with
   age, or is the wrong shade, you can try the automatic contrast
   and colour effects. Both are available from the **Effects –
   Enhance Photo** menu. **Automatic Colour Balance** will allow
   you to move the pointer along a scale to emphasise the warmer
   or cooler colours (see Figure 7.6).

Drag pointer to
increase
warmer tones

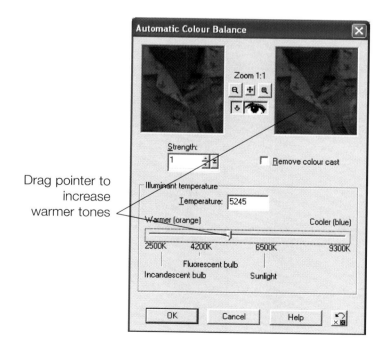

Figure 7.6

Automatic Contrast Enhancement can help you increase the highlights and shadows (see Figure 7.7).

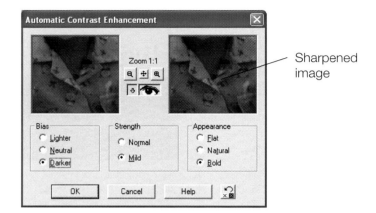

Sharpened image

Figure 7.7

6. When you have made all your changes, save the new image with a different name or in a new location, and decide whether or not to change it to a different file type (such as .jpg) that will save space but may lose a little of the detail. (For example, the above image was 86.5 KB as a JPEG and 1.18MB as a PSP file.)

7. You can now keep the renovated photo on your computer or print it out on specially purchased photographic paper.

8

Finding things on the Web

Once you decide that you want to use your computer for searching the Internet and sending messages, you must register with an Internet Service Provider (ISP). You will need to provide your personal details and choose an identification – your username and password – that will safeguard your settings. The ISP will establish dialling facilities which your computer will be set to dial automatically; will install the latest browser software, such as Internet Explorer or Netscape, needed for viewing Web pages; and will offer you an email address.

There are hundreds of ISPs who offer these services and all the necessary software can be installed via a CD-ROM available from shops, magazines or in the post. Load the disk into your CD-ROM drive and follow the instructions to install the software and register with the ISP. Once you have a connection, you can always change to a different ISP by registering on the new company's Website.

Figure 8.1

Having signed up with an Internet Service Provider (ISP), you should be ready to double-click the Internet Explorer 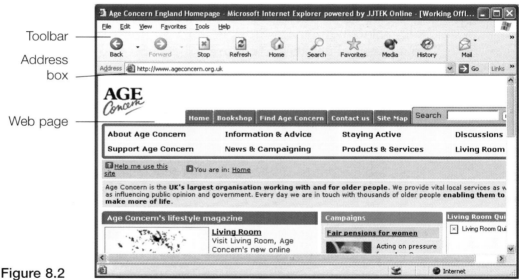 or ISP icon to open your browser window and connect to the World Wide Web. You may like to set the computer to remember your username and password so that connections are quick and easy, or you may have signed up for broadband and will stay connected all the time.

Web pages

Inside the browser window, a colourful Web page of text and pictures should fill the screen.

Toolbar

Address box

Web page

Figure 8.2

Working with the Internet will soon become straightforward. You have several menus and toolbar buttons along the top of the browser window which will be explained later. Most useful are the **Back** and **Forward** buttons: . As you visit new pages, the old ones will still be available. Click **Back** to work back through pages you have visited, or **Forward** to move on again.

Home page

Each time you connect, the same initial Web page will be displayed. This is your home page and is usually a page of information provided by your ISP. You return here each time you click the **Home** button  in your browser window. If it is not a convenient starting point for an Internet session – perhaps you prefer to start by reading the news, checking what's on TV or viewing information from your housing association – you can set any page as your home page.

Type the address of your preferred Web page into the Address box, over the address already showing there, and then press the Enter key or click the button labelled **Go**. When the page appears, open the **Tools** menu and select **Internet Options**.

Figure 8.3

In the **Home page** section, click **Use Current** and then click **OK** to close the window (see Figure 8.4). This page will now open every time you connect to the Internet or click the **Home** button in future.

Click to set page

Confirm settings

Figure 8.4

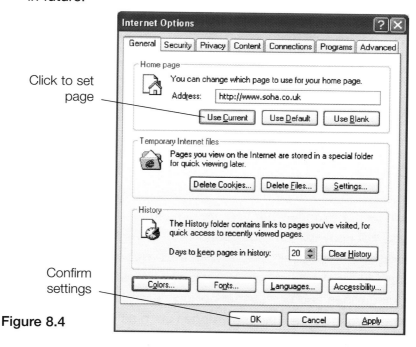

Open new pages

You can open new Web pages in two ways:

a. Type the address of the page into the Address box and press Enter (or click the **Go** button) Address [www.soha.co.uk] ∨ → Go . The address is often referred to as the URL (Uniform Resource Locator) and will have the form www.name.*co.uk* (or *org.uk*, *com*, *ac.uk*, *gov.uk*, etc depending on the type of organisation it is). You may notice that at some stage the letters http:// are added automatically, but these do not need to be typed.

b. Click on the page when the pointer displays a hand 🖑 . This hand appears when it is over a hyperlink that has been embedded in the Web page. These links are commonly used for opening indexes or finding information that readers will want to move to within the Website, and the link text usually changes colour or shows as underlined.

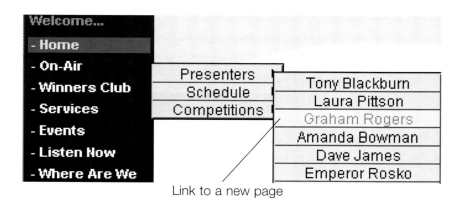

Figure 8.5   Link to a new page

Searching

There is so much information on the World Wide Web that it can be hard to locate exactly what you are looking for. In many cases, you will know which organisation can provide the information and so you will need to visit their Website by typing the address in the Address box. You will see Website addresses listed in magazines and newspapers or on TV, and may already have come across some well-known ones such as www.bbc.co.uk, www.ageconcern.org.uk, www.guardian.co.uk or www.inlandrevenue.gov.uk

The problem comes when you want information that doesn't belong to a single organisation: weather reports, cricket scores, medical information, historical facts, etc. For this reason, special types of Website have been set up known as search engines. Many such Websites are available, including www.google.co.uk, www.altavista.com, and www.yahoo.co.uk

All they offer is a method for searching thousands of different Websites, looking for the specific information you have asked them to find. When the list of sites appears on the page, you can click a link to any one and see if the information you are seeking is provided. In some cases, they also group related Websites together so that you can work through categories such as *Recreation and Leisure – Sport – Tennis – Tennis Clubs* to locate a limited number of relevant Websites already catalogued for you.

When searching, you need to type a word or phrase into a box provided on screen known as the Query or Search box. These are your 'keywords' and the more care you take with them, the more accurate the search results will be. For example, what if you wanted to find recipes for older people who have diabetes? Here is how refining the keywords can result in a shorter, more accurate and manageable list of Websites to visit:

a. *Diabetes recipes (1,280,000 results)*. Websites included many from overseas where recipes used different units of measure and unobtainable products.
b. *Diabetes recipes* **UK** *(31,100)*. UK Websites only, but included many featuring books you would have to buy.
c. *Diabetes recipes UK* **online** *(18,600)*. More helpful, but often aimed at babies and small children.
d. *Diabetes recipes UK online* **for older people** *(2,490)*. The most relevant and manageable list.

If you are unsure of a spelling, or want to find a range of related Websites, you can use the asterix * to replace parts of a word.

For example, entering *post** might pick up Websites featuring information on postage, postcards, posters and fence posts.

One problem often encountered when searching for information and following up one of the listed sites is that the exact word or phrase may be lost in the heart of a detailed Web page. If you are viewing a Web page but cannot find the information easily, open the **Edit** menu and select **Find (on This Page)**.

Figure 8.6

Type your keyword(s) into the box and click **Find Next**. A matching word should be highlighted on the page and you can keep clicking **Find Next** until the section that interests you is located.

Figure 8.7

Project 10

Use a search engine to find a map of Age Concern offices and print a copy

1. With your computer connected to the Internet and the browser window open, type the address of the Google search engine (www.google.co.uk) in the Address box and press the Enter key.

Click for picture search

Query box

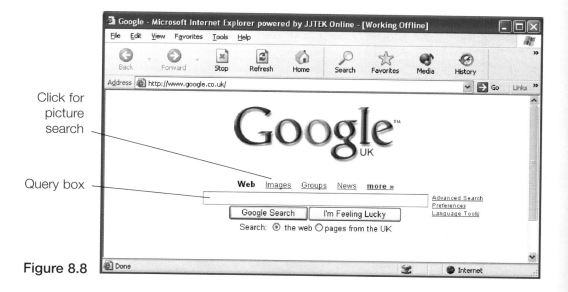

Figure 8.8

2. You will see several underlined labels as well as the empty Query box. Leave the page at **Web** for this search, as you need to locate a Website that provides search boxes and facilities for viewing the map. For different searches, you can first click **Images** or **News** in order to limit your search to pictures or the latest news.

3. There are many Websites providing street maps, so type the search words *street maps* into the Query box and press Enter to display a list of map sites. Make sure that you also click the **pages from the UK** circular (radio) button (see Figure 8.9), or type *UK* in the Query box before searching, in order to limit the search to companies providing maps of the UK or part of the UK.

Figure 8.9

4. In a few seconds, you will see a list of pages. Each one may display a brief description of its contents and the date it was last updated, and has a clickable title to take you to the Website. At the top of the page you will see the number of Websites located with this search ('hits'), although those at the end of the list will probably be a poor match for your keywords.

Relevant sites located —

Click to visit Website

Click scroll bar arrow to reveal further sites down the page —

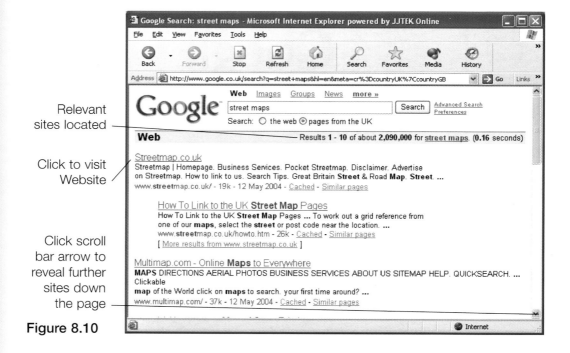

Figure 8.10

5. Click the link to the first Website in the list and use the boxes on the page to enter part of the address – postcode, street name or other identifier; for example *1268 London Road* or *SW16 4ER*. Click the correct circular (radio) button and then click **Search**.

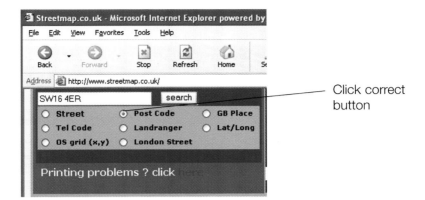

Click correct
button

Figure 8.11

6. The map will slowly be revealed and you can drag the scroll
bars up or down, click a directional arrow or change the
magnification until you can see your street clearly. It is identified
by an arrow in some systems and a red circle in others.

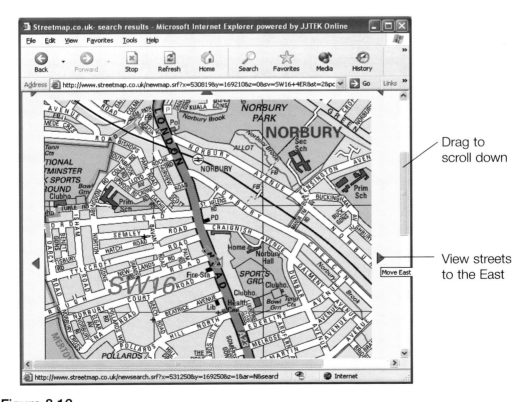

Drag to
scroll down

View streets
to the East

Figure 8.12

7. If the map is not helpful, click your **Back** button to return to the search list and visit another Website.

8. Once you find a satisfactory map, you can print a copy to keep. If there is a link to a printable version, click this first as it will remove the advertisements etc.

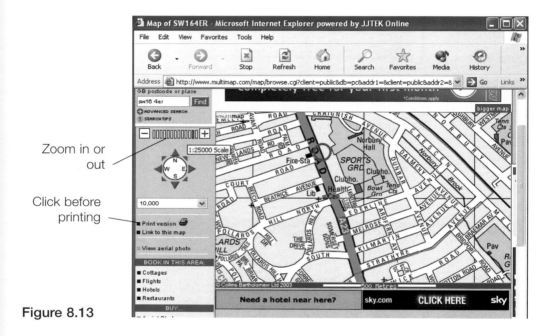

Zoom in or out

Click before printing

Figure 8.13

9. Now is the time to disconnect if you are paying for each minute online. Double-click the computer symbol on your Taskbar and click the **Disconnect** button. The map will stay on screen until you close the browser window.

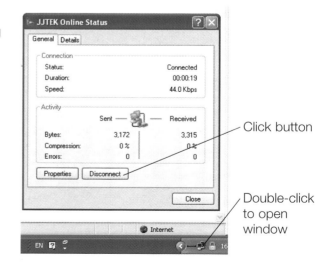

Click button

Double-click to open window

Figure 8.14

10. Printing Web pages is straightforward – simply click your **Print** button to print a copy. However, a Web 'page' may be longer than the usual word-processed page, so make sure that you have enough paper if you want all the information, or limit your printing to the first page. Open **File – Print** and set to print 1 page only.

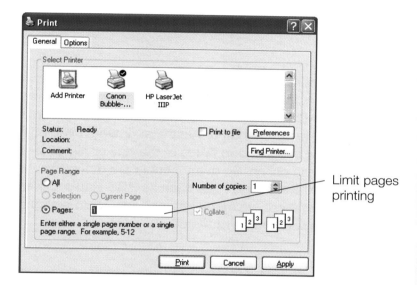

Limit pages printing

Figure 8.15

9

Radio online

Do you fancy listening to digital broadcasts without buying a new radio; would you like to hear programmes you missed the first time round; have you wondered what type of programmes people listen to in America or Australia; or would you enjoy music or local news at odd times of the day or night? If so, you can now tune in online. So many people are doing this that alongside well-known services such as BBC Radio 4 or the World Service, there are many Internet-only radio stations catering for a wide range of tastes.

Figure 9.1

Your Windows XP machine should have a sound card and the necessary software, in the form of Windows Media Player, to listen to most of the radio output. However, some services may require different software, such as RealPlayer or RealOnePlayer, that are available free to download from Websites such as the BBC at www.bbc.co.uk/radio

Figure 9.2

You may need to take out a subscription for some content and, in the case of Digital Audio Broadcasting (DAB), you may also have to buy extra equipment.

Finding radio Websites

You may know some sites that you want to visit, such as the BBC, Radio Now or Classic Gold, but your player offers a good range of stations as a starting point. Open Internet Explorer, go online and click the **Media** toolbar button to open the player on the left of the screen.

Select **Radio Guide** from the **Media Options** menu, or click if the link is visible, and you will display a list of stations including the World Service that you can listen to.

Select station

Music stored
on your
computer

Click for guide

Figure 9.3

Click any station name to offer further details and a **Play** button,
or to go to their Website.

Figure 9.4

Each Website is organised differently, but there should be links
to different programmes or types of music. Manoeuvre through
the menus and click any link that says **Listen** or **Play Now**.

Figure 9.5

(published by permission of www.radio-now.co.uk)

Even if you launch the Player in full-screen mode, you can always minimise the window and continue working on your computer and the station will play in the background.

Minimise

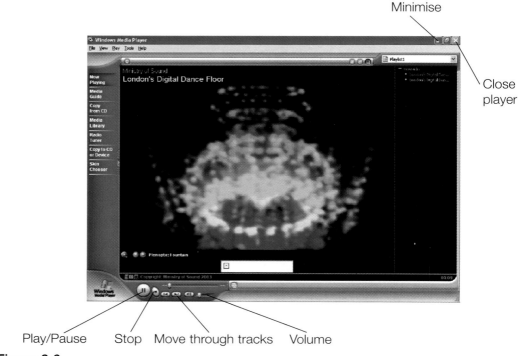

Close
player

Play/Pause   Stop   Move through tracks   Volume

Figure 9.6

Project 11

Bookmark favourite radio Website addresses

Once you find a radio station offering a choice of programmes or music of special interest, you will want to keep the Website address handy. Although recently listened to stations will be added to the Radio Guide, and you can click a link labelled **Add to My Stations**, you may want to group particular types of station and otherwise manage the links, or visit the Website without opening the Media Player. One way is to add stations to a folder specially set aside to store Web page links known as Favourites.

1. With the Web page open in your browser window, click the **Favorites** button or select it from the menu bar. This will display a list of folders that have already been created.

2. First check that the company delivers to your postcode area. You will now have to register and provide your contact details, so click the link and complete the form. Each time you visit the site you must enter your user name and password, but you may be able to set your computer to remember these details to save typing them each time.

Figure 10.2   Register   Check postcode

3. Most retailers offer the chance to book a delivery day and time before you start shopping, so click the link and then click on the day and time to book a slot.

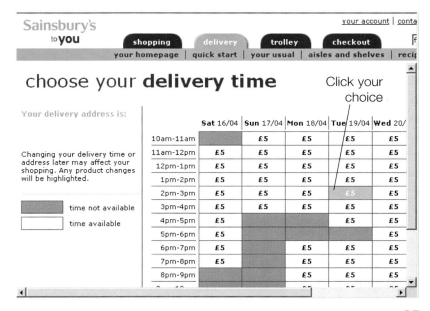

Figure 10.3

4. You can shop in two ways: type the name of the item in a search box and click **Find** or browse the 'aisles' (ie click a top-level category of food types and work down to your chosen items).

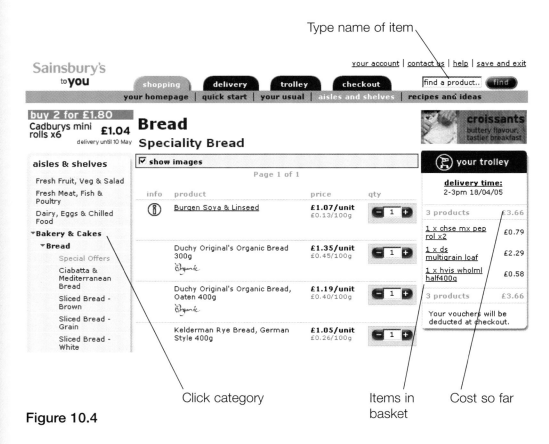

Type name of item

Click category

Items in basket

Cost so far

Figure 10.4

5. For any item you wish to buy, check it shows the correct weight or number of packs, etc. and change these where necessary by clicking the + or – buttons. This will add or remove the item from your basket/trolley. Sometimes you can click an **Info** button to display further details. The basket will remain visible on screen.

6. At any time, you can cancel or add items by clicking the trolley tab and updating the number of items you wanted to order.

Click to show trolley

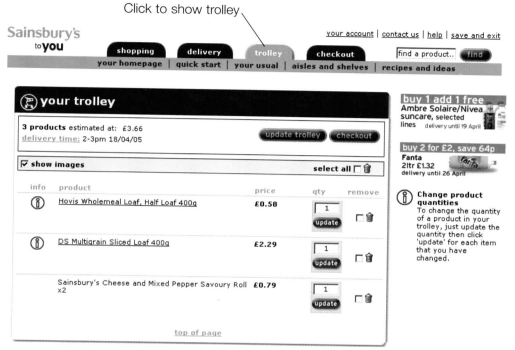

Figure 10.5

7. At the end of your shopping, click **Checkout** to pay.

8. Enter your credit card details and the number on any vouchers you might have been sent. You should see two signs that the Website is secure for making payments: the address will begin with http**s**:// and a padlock will be visible at the bottom of the screen (see Figure 10.6).

Figure 10.6

9. Having completed all the boxes, confirm your purchase and, if you want to, print out a copy of your order. You should receive confirmation of the order by email and can then look forward to your groceries being delivered in a few days' time.

10. If you shop regularly, you will soon save time using the shortcuts offered. For example, you can view your last list or regular items (your usual) or jot down a list of general items on a memo pad (quick start) and choose from just these, which can make Internet shopping quicker than ever.

11

Comparing prices

You can use the Web to check the prices of anything from airline tickets to garden tools, mobile phones or cauliflowers. However, it takes practice and patience to end up with the very best deal. As well as using common search engines, there are Websites set up specifically to compare prices. These can be very useful as a starting point but should never be relied on completely – that's because they may not sample all possible sites, they may not include hidden costs such as delivery, and they may be sponsored by certain manufacturers which can bias their results.

Project 13

Find the cheapest route-planning software

If you make numerous car journeys, it can be helpful to use a program on your computer to work out the quickest route. As well as the online services provided by the AA and RAC, there are a number of route-planning applications available. Although this book is not recommending any particular product, we will use the example of Microsoft AutoRoute 2004 to try and find the cheapest place to buy a copy.

1. When you enter the route planner's title into a search engine query box, two Websites are likely to be listed in the results: DealTime and Kelkoo. These are comparison websites and so are worth visiting.
2. DealTime lists 10 copies of the route planner (see Figure 11.1).

Figure 11.1

3. Clicking the **Price** heading sorts the stores in order of cost (see Figure 11.2).

Sorted by cost —

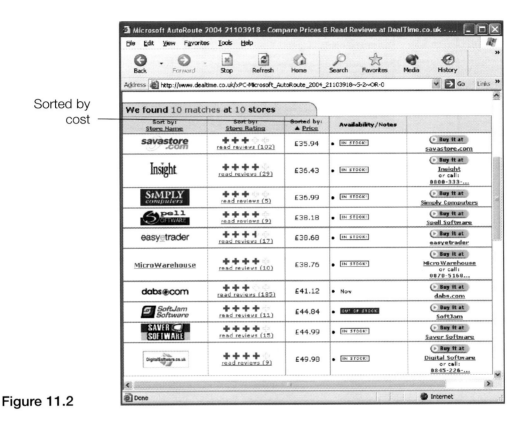

Figure 11.2

4. If you want to buy what appears to be the cheapest software, click the **Buy it at** button to open up the first store's Website. In this example it shows the price at Savastore.com with and without VAT, but no delivery costs (see Figure 11.3).

Figure 11.3

5. Click the **Buy now** button to move on to the next window. You will now see that the final price has jumped from £35.94 to £40.35 after delivery has been added, which may not make it such a good bargain.

			Unit Price	Discount	Total
Current Balance 0 savapoints		**Points in Basket** 30 savapoints	**Balance after Purchase** 30 savapoints		
Qty	**Description**				
1	Autoroute 2004		£30.59	£0.00	£30.59

recalculate - Click if you have changed any quantities

Approximate basket weight: 0.1kg

- Remove Item

Subtotal:	£30.59
Delivery:	*£3.75
Surcharges:	*£0.00
VAT:	£6.01
Total:	£40.35

« more shopping...   empty   place order

delivery & insurance matrix

Order Value / Weight	>0.5kg	>5kg	>10kg	>20kg	>35kg	+35kg
up to £30	£1.75	£3.99	£4.00	£5.50	£7.95	£8.25
up to £125	£3.75	£3.99	£4.50	£4.95	£8.25	£8.50
up to £350	£4.15	£4.50	£4.99	£5.50	£8.50	£8.75
up to £600	£4.59	£5.00	£5.50	£5.99	£8.50	£8.75
£600+	£5.99	£7.00	£7.49	£7.99	£8.50	£8.75

* Carriage charge shown is based on delivery to UK mainland. The actual carriage charge will be shown prior to you confirming the order. Click here to see details of carriage charges.

Figure 11.4

6. If you return to DealTime, you can follow links to the other stores listed and will find that delivery costs range from £5 to £20.

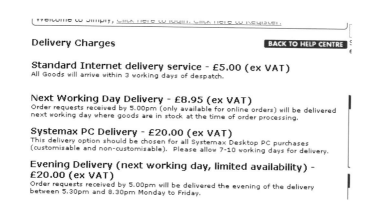

Welcome to Simply, Click here to login. Click here to Register.

Delivery Charges   BACK TO HELP CENTRE

Standard Internet delivery service - £5.00 (ex VAT)
All Goods will arrive within 3 working days of despatch.

Next Working Day Delivery - £8.95 (ex VAT)
Order requests received by 5.00pm (only available for online orders) will be delivered next working day where goods are in stock at the time of order processing.

Systemax PC Delivery - £20.00 (ex VAT)
This delivery option should be chosen for all Systemax Desktop PC purchases (customisable and non-customisable). Please allow 7-10 working days for delivery.

Evening Delivery (next working day, limited availability) - £20.00 (ex VAT)
Order requests received by 5.00pm will be delivered the evening of the delivery between 5.30pm and 8.30pm Monday to Friday.

Figure 11.5

7. Following the Kelkoo link may be more helpful as this Website includes postage costs in its initial listings.

Figure 11.6

8. However, Savastore is not listed, even though it was still the cheapest after delivery charges had been taken into account.

9. Even more annoying is the fact that neither comparison site lists the Internet bookshop Amazon. This company also sells a wide range of electronic and software products and, at the time of writing, if you spend more than £19, delivers them free. This makes today's price at Amazon of £39.99, including delivery, the cheapest to date.

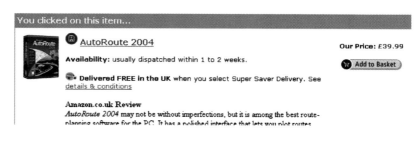

Figure 11.7

10. One conclusion that can be drawn from this exercise is that you need to become familiar with specialist companies that have a good reputation for low-priced products such as Amazon, Tesco, WHSmith (which delivers items free for collection at your local store) and Argos. Visit them *as well* as those recommended by general search engines or comparison Websites before making a purchase.

12

Downloads

As well as information, games, chat rooms, tutorials and things to buy, the Internet offers useful programs that will make your computer safer and easier to use. Many of these programs are available free, and you can save them onto your computer through a process known as 'downloading'.

In particular, you may want to download:

Drivers: this is software that enables you to use items such as graphics cards, printers and scanners. Although you will have installed the original software when you first bought your new piece of equipment, the manufacturers are continually making improvements so that now and again it is a good idea to move up to newer versions, to make sure you run the equipment as efficiently as possible. Drivers are free to download from the manufacturers' own Websites. There are 'generic' versions available that work with a range of similar equipment, but the ideal is to download programs specifically aimed at your make and model. If you can, keep a note of all the details when you first buy hardware items, so you will have these to hand when required.

Utilities: there are a range of programs available that make life easier. For example they can:

- help clean up your computer (eg Easy Remover Pro);
- allow you to read certain types of file (eg Adobe Acrobat Reader);

- make downloading faster (eg Fresh Download);
- work as an alternative browser to Internet Explorer (eg Mozilla); or
- prevent annoying pop-up adverts appearing every few minutes (eg Pop-Up Stopper).

Anti-virus software: Some people try to spread programs known as viruses over the Internet that cause computers to crash or send out thousands of meaningless emails. For home users, they are often more of a nuisance than anything else, but you will want to prevent them gaining access to your machine. The software needed will check for viruses whenever you start your computer, receive emails or spend time on the Internet. Commonly bought programs are produced by Norton and McAfee, but you can also find free software. As new viruses are produced on a regular basis, you will find that you need to update the software regularly. Most anti-virus programs include a button to click labelled **Update** that will automatically connect you to the software company Website and download and install the latest version on your computer.

Project 14

Download the virus checker AVG and use it to scan your computer

A good quality, free program for checking for viruses is produced by Grisoft. This is called AVG and can be located at its Website (www.grisoft.com).

1. On the page, click the link to the free version (see Figure 12.1).

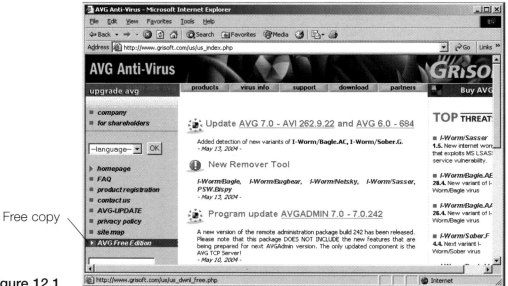

Figure 12.1

2. You will need to register with the Website as the serial number that allows you to install the program will only be sent to you via email (see Figure 12.2).

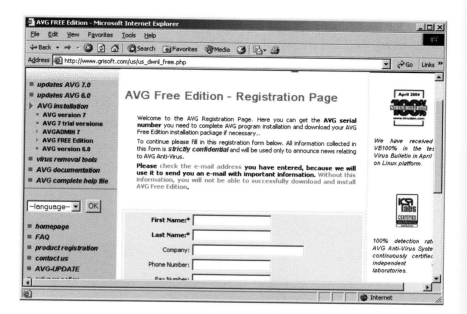

Figure 12.2

3. Having completed registration, the AVG program you want to download will be displayed on the screen and may start downloading automatically. If not, click the **Download** button to start the process.

File to download

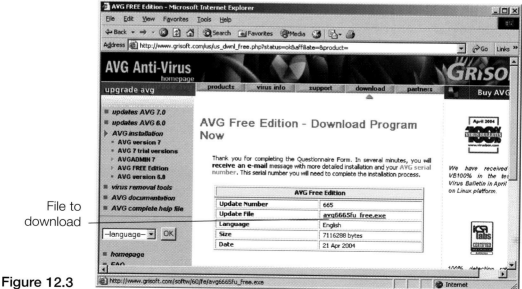

Figure 12.3

4. Check where the program is going to be saved to, as you will need to locate it to install it properly once it is on your computer. One option is to save it to your Desktop, where it will be clearly visible. Once the process starts, you will see a window showing the progress of the download and how long it will take. You can carry out other tasks on your computer, but must not disconnect from the Internet until you reach the end of the process. To help remind you that the process is complete, click in the box to specify that the window closes once download is complete (see Figure 12.4).

Click if you want the
window to close

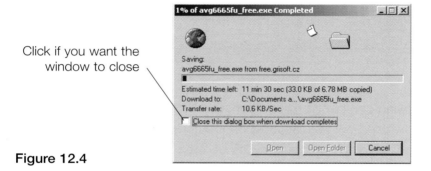

Figure 12.4

5. The file will be visible on your Desktop, if saved there, 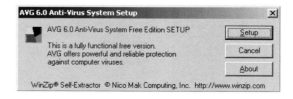 or you will need to find it within your computer.
6. Wait for the email containing the serial number to arrive. Write down the number and then double-click the file to start the set-up process. Unless you have a good reason, accept the suggested file name and locations that are offered as this will mean updating should be straightforward.

Figure 12.5

7. At the appropriate time, enter your serial number in the box provided. When set-up is complete, your computer will restart so that all the necessary settings can be confirmed. You can then use the program to check your computer or to download the latest updates over the Internet. The colourful icon for the anti-virus program will be added to your taskbar and the software will check your computer every time you start a new session or receive emails. You can even set a date for regular sweeps of your computer just to be on the safe side.

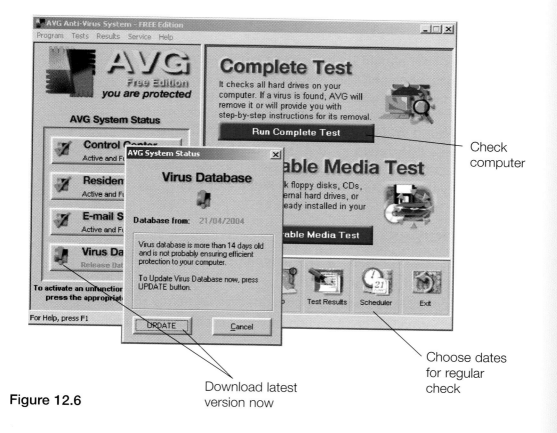

Figure 12.6

Check computer

Download latest version now

Choose dates for regular check

13

Emails and attachments

No computer user should be without an email address. You can then send messages and files around the world in just a few seconds, at minimum cost. During the process of registering with an Internet Service Provider (ISP) for dial-up connections to view the World Wide Web, you will have created an email address. Some ISPs, such as AOL, provide their own email software, but in most cases you can use a program already installed on your computer such as Outlook Express .

Email address

Your address will be made up of a username or ID, @ and then the name of your ISP – for example *Username@compuserve.com* or *Username@btinternet.co.uk* The username is normally a combination of your initials or first name and surname, perhaps with the addition of a number, and is chosen by you during the registration process. As someone else may already have chosen your preferred username, have several others ready in case you need to suggest a suitable alternative.

Web-based email

If you don't have your own computer or software such as Outlook Express, but want to send and receive emails using public computers in libraries or colleges, you can register for a free Web address at Websites such as www.yahoo.co.uk, www.hotmail.com or www.go4.it Once registered, you can log on from any computer whenever you access the World Wide Web and use your message system online.

To register, you will need to provide both a username and a secret password known only to you. It is *very* important that you remember the exact wording (and case) of your username and password as you will need to type them each time you want to use the service.

Project 15

Register for a Web-based email address

Web-based email systems work in a similar way, so here is how to register with one: go4.it

1. Type in *www.go4.it* in the Address box in your browser and then press Enter or click **Go**.

2. Click the **Webmail** link or the shortcut offered to new users (see Figure 13.1).

Click a link

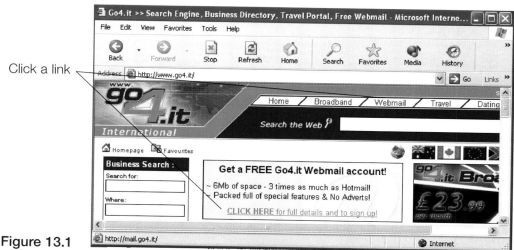

Figure 13.1

3. Read the information and then click to register. You will be presented with an online form and must complete all the boxes showing a red * (see Figure 13.2).

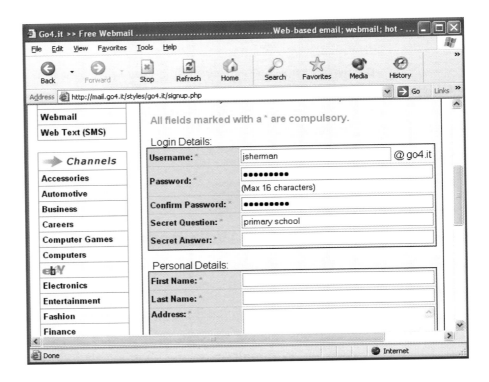

Figure 13.2

The password will display a series of *** or ••• so that no-one standing nearby can see what you have typed. The secret question is a prompt and it is up to you what you put in the question and answer boxes. If you forget your password, being able to type the correct answer to the question may mean you are still allowed access to your mail.

4. After completing the form and submitting it, you will be told that you have been registered. You can now sign in each time you want to use the service by completing the username and password boxes, and clicking the **Login** button in the Members area.

Webmail

Members
Login:

Username: _____ @go4.it

Password: _____

Login

Not yet a registered user? Click Here!
Get your FREE email address - yourname@Go4.it!

Figure 13.3

Working with Outlook Express

Open Outlook Express by double-clicking the icon [icon]. You will see the page shown below in Figure 13.4, but you can set the system to start in your mailbox each time you open it in future. If you are not on broadband and your computer tries to connect to the Internet when you open Outlook Express, click the **Work offline** button. It will save your phone bill if you only connect when you want to send or receive emails.

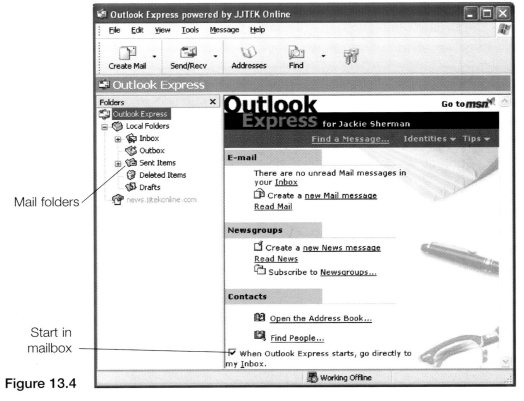

Mail folders

Start in mailbox

Figure 13.4

Folders

On the left you can see the folders in which messages will be stored. Click any one to see its contents on the right. The folders are:

Inbox: all new messages arrive here and the number of unread messages is shown in brackets next to the folder name. Double-click any message to read it in its own window.

Outbox: a temporary storage folder where messages wait until you connect to the Internet and send them.

Sent Items: copies of all messages that have been sent are stored here.

Drafts: if you want to continue working on a message, save it here temporarily.

Deleted Items: messages you don't want to keep are stored here until you choose to empty this folder.

Creating a Message

Click the **Create Mail** button and complete the boxes in the new message window that opens:

To: the full email address of anyone you are writing to.

Cc: the full email address of anyone who should receive a copy of your message, including any attachments.

Subject: a summary of the contents of your message.

Figure 13.5

Type your message in the main window and then decide which of the following actions is appropriate:

Click the **Send** button to move your message to the Outbox and start the dial-up process to connect to the Internet. If you are online, the message will be sent straightaway.

- **File – Send Later** will place the message in your Outbox but not start connecting. You can write several more messages and send them all at the same time when you have finished.
- **File – Save** will place the message in your Drafts folder, to continue working on at a later date.

If you previously delayed sending messages but you are now ready to do so, click the **Send/Receive** button in the main window to connect to the Internet and send all the messages in your Outbox. You will also receive any messages that have been sent to you in the meantime.

Project 16

Send a picture as an email attachment

If you took a picture of your pet as described in Project 5, you might like to follow these instructions to send it to a friend or relative by email.

1. Write your message and then click the **Attach** button showing a paperclip (see Figure 13.6), or open the **Insert** menu and select **File Attachment**.

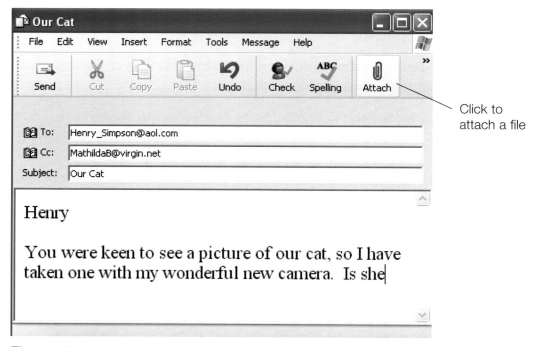

Click to attach a file

Figure 13.6

2. You will open your computer folders. Browse through the files on your computer and when you find the file, select it and then click the **Attach** button.

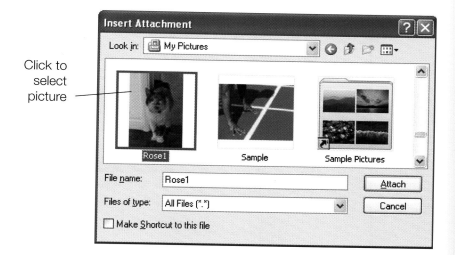

Click to
select
picture

Figure 13.7

3. Back in your message, you will see the file in a new **Attach** box (see Figure 13.8).

To: Henry_Simpson@aol.com

Cc: MathildaB@virgin.net

Subject: Our Cat

Attach: Rose1.JPG (37.2 KB)

Figure 13.8

Henry

You can repeat the process to add further files to the message, and then send it as normal.

4. If the file you want to send is very large, it is a good idea to compress it first, so that it takes up less space. Windows XP compresses files by a process known as 'zipping'. To zip a file, first locate the file by opening My Computer and then opening the folders inside until you can see the image file name. *Right-*click the name and select **Send To – Compressed (zipped) Folder** (see Figure 13.9).

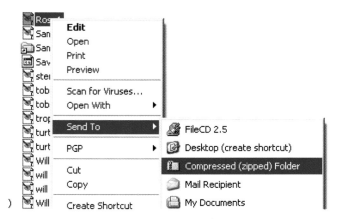

Figure 13.9

A new folder displaying a zip will appear at the end of the list of files ▣Rose1. It will have the same name as the image file and will contain it in a compressed format. This folder can be attached to an email in exactly the same way as a normal file.

As long as your recipient has Windows XP or a program that works with zipped files, such as WinZip, they can double-click the file to open it again.

5. If you receive a message containing an attachment it will display a paperclip when it first arrives in the Inbox. ℗ 📬
6. The file will be displayed in the Attach box when you open the message fully, so double-click to open it. You will be offered the option to save the file to disk rather than open it directly, as it may contain viruses (see Figure 13.10). This will enable you to run your virus checker to make sure it is safe.

Figure 13.10

14

Communicating on the Web

As well as emails that are sent to people in the form of electronic 'letters', there are other ways to communicate via the Internet. The two most common are: chat rooms, which are equivalent to real-time conversations; and forums or message boards, which can be thought of as a cross between emailing a large group of strangers and pinning up notices on a notice board. If you want to communicate specifically with older people, Age Concern has forums on its main Website and a chat room named the Baby Boomer Bistro.

For all these systems, you are required to register and provide basic details about yourself. You must also agree to rules governing such things as the language you use, so that no-one is upset by what takes place. Some systems have a moderator who keeps an eye on proceedings, but this is not always the case.

Much is heard about the dangers of chat rooms, simply because no-one knows the true identity of anyone using them. Instead, you are asked to choose a nickname by which you will be known. For this reason, you should take great care and never reveal too much personal information about yourself.

Chat rooms

When you click a link to a chat room you will be online at the same time as everyone else taking part in the discussion. (If no-one else appears, there is nothing much you can do except try again another day.) Having made the link, your nickname will be revealed to the other users and you can join in the conversation whenever you like by typing your comments in a small box below the screen and then pressing Enter. Your text will soon appear on a new line. You can exit the room at any time.

One slightly disconcerting aspect of chat rooms is that there is always a small delay between typing and seeing your words on screen, so you may find yourself replying to a topic that has moved on!

Forums

Forums and message boards do not require you to be present at any particular time. When you read a message that you want to reply to, click the **Reply** button, type your comments and then send them in. Writing replies in this way on the Web is known as 'posting' and next time you visit the forum you will see your reply and perhaps others that have been added in the meantime. Messages are normally left on the board for days or months and in many cases contain helpful advice and tips from experts on the topic of the forum. Examples of forums on the Age Concern Website include books, gardening and IT.

Project 17

Join in a Baby Boomer Bistro chat room

1. Go to the Website at www.babyboomerbistro.org.uk

First-time
users need
to register

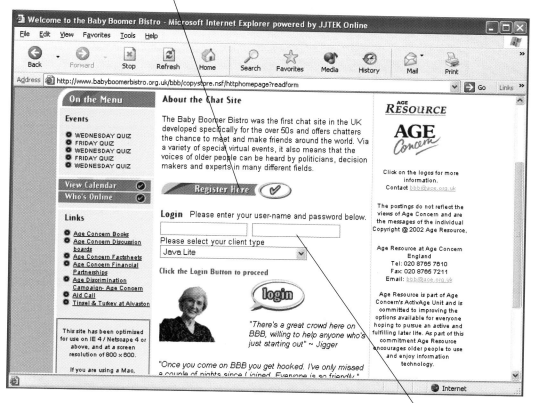

Login on
subsequent visits

Figure 14.1

2. You will need to register, so click the link (see Figure 14.1) and complete the details (see Figure 14.2). If you make any mistakes, you will be directed back to complete those particular boxes again.

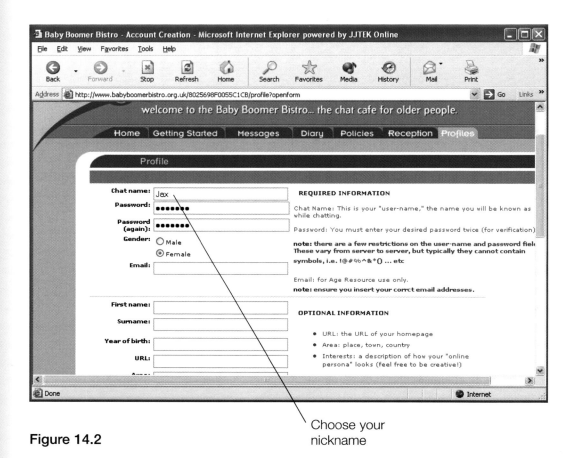

Figure 14.2

Choose your nickname

3. Once registered, you will need to login by typing your chat nickname and password into the appropriate boxes. This is the process you must repeat every time you want to chat in the future.

4. Once inside the Website, you will see that there are several 'rooms' to visit. Different people will get together in these, perhaps establishing a certain style of conversation or discussing particular topics, and so it is a good idea to visit each one and watch the current conversation unfold for a while.

5. As anyone joining a room is identified to the others, you will probably be welcomed. Type your reply in the box under the window and press Enter to add it to the conversation.

People currently in the room

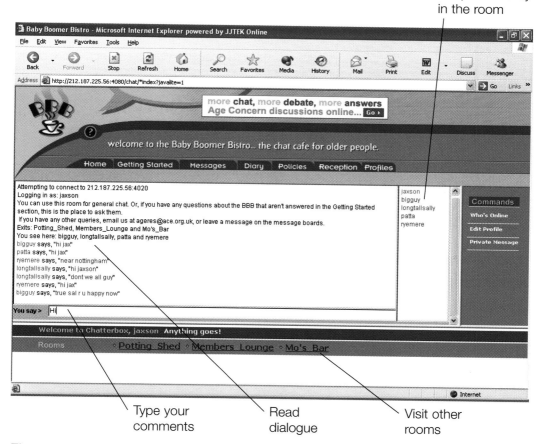

Type your comments

Read dialogue

Visit other rooms

Figure 14.3

Project 18

Add comments to an Age Concern forum

1. Visit the main Website by entering www.ageconcern.org.uk in your browser address box. On the page, click the **Discussions** link.

Join a forum

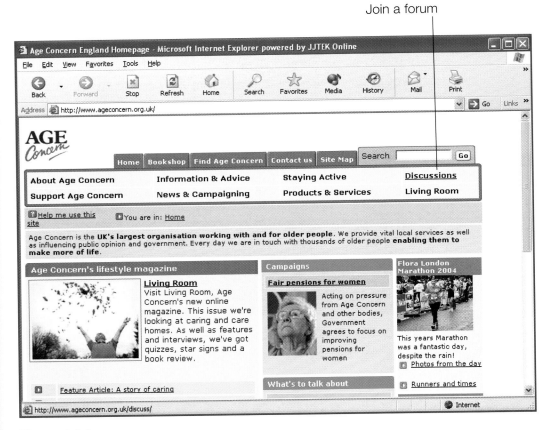

Figure 14.4

2. Once again, you must first register and choose an appropriate nickname so that you are able to login. Although you can read the messages without doing so, you will not be able to reply or start any new discussions.

3. Look at the subjects listed on the page and click any tab to view them in more detail.

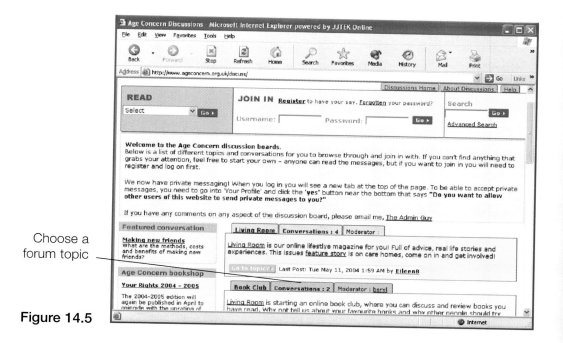

Choose a forum topic

Figure 14.5

4. You will see how many messages each topic has attracted so far, and can click the name to view these. They are arranged by date and you can read through them all or click any page number.

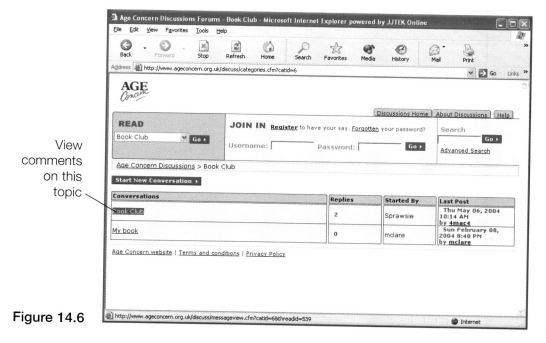

View comments on this topic

Figure 14.6

5. If you see a comment to which you would like to reply, or you have a question to ask, click the **Post Your Reply** button and then type in your message in the box provided, before submitting it for publication on the forum.

Add a comment

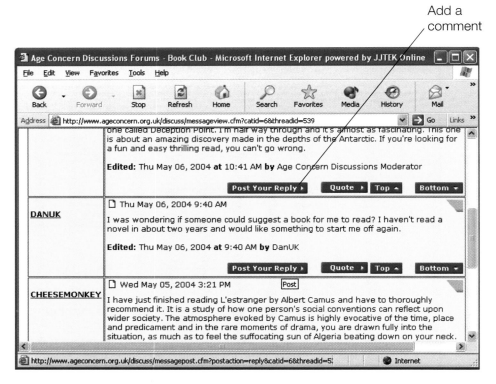

Figure 14.7

Online games

If you like playing certain games like cribbage, scrabble or chess, type the name into a search engine Query box to find out where they can be downloaded or played online. However, if you are not dedicated to a specific game, visit one of the many Websites – such as www.realarcade.com, games.yahoo.com or www.coffeebreakarcade.com/games/ – that offer the chance to play a wide range of games including fantasy, puzzle, card or board games. Many sites also provide chat room facilities so that you will see the nicknames of other people playing and can chat to them during your games session.

Project 19

Play a game of Word Whomp online

This game is similar to another you will find on many game Websites called Text Twist. It requires you to make words from a limited number of letters, playing against the clock, and you can ask the computer to reorder the letters to help you think of new words. Click the letters to add them to the grid, and click Enter to submit the word. As you progress, you work up to harder levels.

1. One gaming Website that offers the chance to play this game is www.pogo.com, so visit the site and register with your basic details and a nickname for others to use. You will see details of its range of games on the main home page (see Figure 15.1).

Figure 15.1

2. Click any game and you will be offered a list of rooms in which to play, as well as the possibility to go to one containing people of a similar age. Click any link to go to that room and wait for the game to load. Unfortunately, you will have to view an advertisement each time you do so, but these help pay for the upkeep of the Website.

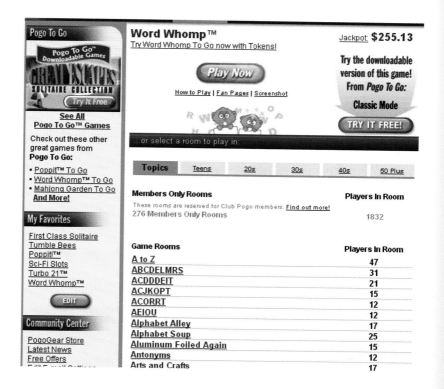

Figure 15.2

3. Once in the room, if the game is new to you, find out how to play by clicking the link to the rules.

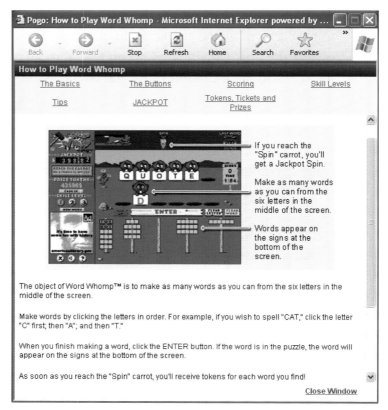

Figure 15.3

4. When you are ready, return to the room and start playing.

Click letter
to add it to
a grid

Words
completed
so far

Figure 15.4

16

Auctions

Nowadays, the pleasure and excitement of visiting a car boot sale has been superseded by taking part in an Internet auction. There are several auction Websites, but the most famous by far is www.eBay.co.uk It works on the principle that one person's rubbish is another's treasure, and you can buy anything from antiques to clothes, furniture or jewellery.

However, people will only buy from sellers who have received positive feedback about their activities. Once a seller is given negative feedback, perhaps because the goods didn't turn up or were not as described, it will be hard for them to regain the confidence of other customers. It is therefore reasonably safe to take part, as long as you use your common sense:

a. Don't respond to emails sent to you after you lose an item in an auction on eBay, offering something similar – you will not have eBay's protection.

b. Set up an international payment system, for example using PayPal (see page 128), and use a credit card wherever possible, so that you are more likely to receive compensation if your goods are not supplied.

c. No site can ever be 100% safe, so take great care if purchasing expensive items – losing £10 may be bearable but losing £1,000 may not.

d. Some people set up fake Websites that look as if they are genuine auctions – make sure the appropriate questions and screens are offered and, if you are unhappy about anything, don't continue with a purchase but send details to eBay for it to investigate.

Project 20

Buy a second-hand audio CD on eBay

1. Go to the Website and either type in a keyword in the **Search** box (such as a singer or band name), or first click the **Music** category in the left-hand column to search within this.

Use keyword search ————

Search category

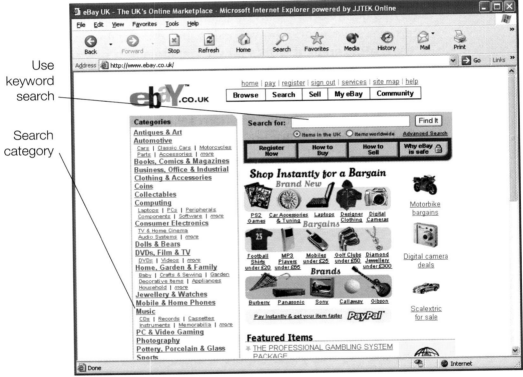

Figure 16.1

2. After clicking the **Find it** or **Show items** button, a list of all related items currently for sale will appear on screen. Some will have pictures of the object and all will display the price. They will either show when they were listed or, if you click the **Time Listed** button, how long you have left to bid. Most items are on sale for 7 or 10 days.

Keywords

When listed

Price

Figure 16.2

3. To see further details of any items of interest, click the blue, underlined title. You will find details of the seller, a fuller description of the item, postage costs and how many people have already bid for it. You can even send an email to the seller if you have a question about the item.

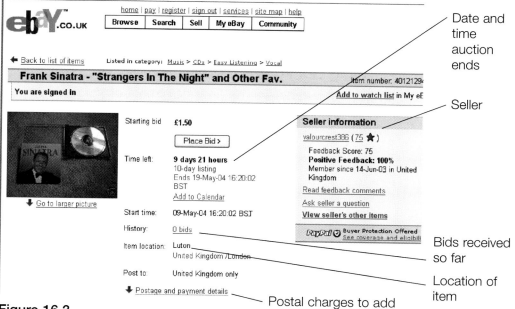

Date and time auction ends

Seller

Bids received so far

Location of item

Postal charges to add

Figure 16.3

4. If you want to buy anything, you have to be registered on the Website. Click the register link and complete the online form. You *must* have a valid email address (that is not a free one such as a Hotmail account) as you will be sent messages telling you the state of your bid and, at the end of the auction, if you have won as well as how to pay.

5. All eBay users have an ID so that their details are not revealed on screen to the general public and to allow access to their own account.

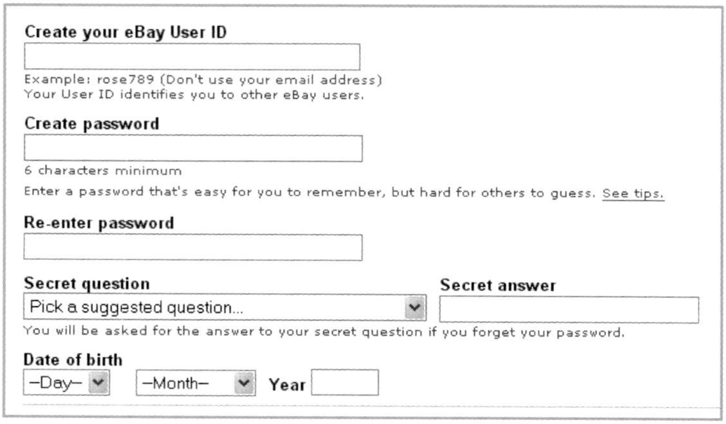

Figure 16.4

6. When you find an item you want to buy, click the **Place Bid** button on the details page. If you don't want to wait for the end of the auction and you are offered an acceptable price at which you can buy straightaway, click the **Buy It Now** button. Not all items have this option, but it can save the disappointment of losing out to someone who puts in a higher bid than you.

Figure 16.5

7. Bidding involves entering the *maximum* price you are prepared to pay. The Website will enter the lowest possible bid and, as others join in, will continue to bid on your behalf automatically over the next hours or days up to your maximum or until the auction ends. You will either win the item or lose it to someone who enters a price higher than your maximum.

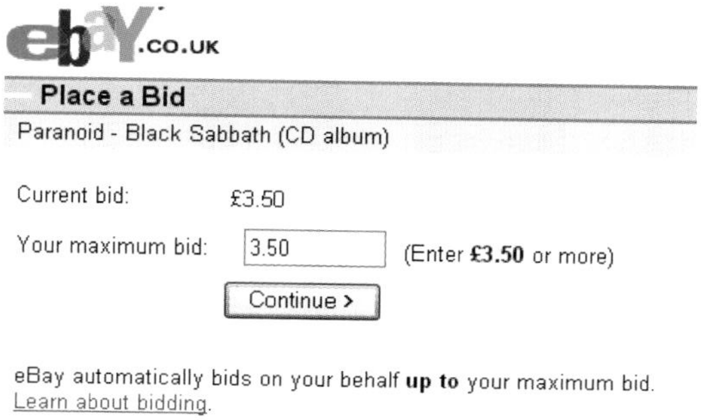

Figure 16.6

8. Having agreed the bid, you will see a confirmation that you are currently the highest bidder and you will receive an email to this effect.

Figure 16.7

9. Near the end of the auction, go online if you want to watch the prices change – you will need to click your **Refresh** button  to see the latest entries. If no-one outbids you, you will be notified that you have won and will need to pay on the Website. A link to the page for payment and feedback will be included in your final email as well on the site.

Figure 16.8

10. If you have not registered with PayPal, now is a good time to do so. Click the link to sign up and select the appropriate type of account before completing the email and credit card details. If you want to sell goods on a regular basis, you may prefer a business account that allows you to accept credit card payments.

   You will need to choose a password to allow you to access your account each time you buy or if you want to change any details. The money for any goods you buy will now be taken from your bank by PayPal and sent to the seller's bank without you needing to type in your credit card details again.

Figure 16.9

11. Although it is not strictly necessary, some people contact the seller directly, to provide fuller details for the delivery of their goods.

Project 21

Sell an old video on eBay

1. Click the **Sell** link on the opening screen and login with your username and password. You must be registered with eBay before you can sell anything. Check the **Sell at online Auction button** and click **Continue**.

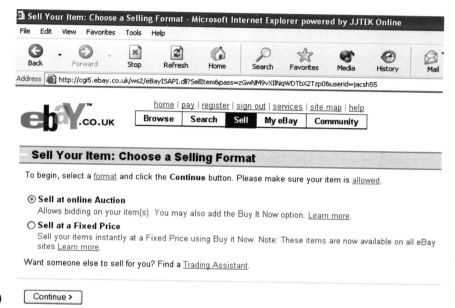

Figure 16.10

2. Many people search through categories of items for sale, so select the most appropriate category for your item. Either click a name in the list or type in details of your item in the keywords box (see Figure 16.11).

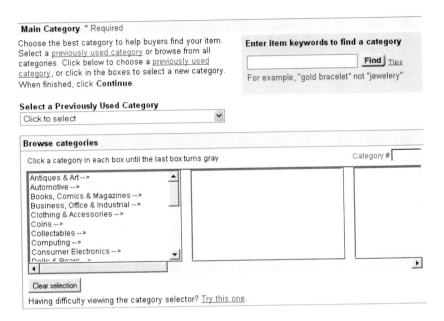

Figure 16.11

3. The page shown in Figure 16.12 is the place to describe your item in detail. The title will appear in blue, underlined text on the main page when people search, so make sure it is clear what is being sold. Some sections are included in the basic price, but you can pay for extra features, such as a subtitle if you want to make your advertisement stand out even more.

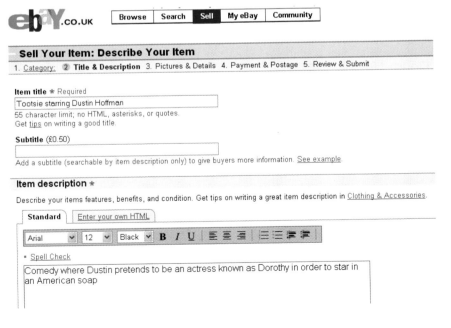

Figure 16.12

4. Decide on the minimum price you will accept and set this as the reserve, if you would be unhappy letting your item go for less. You must also 'start' the bidding at a lower figure to get the ball rolling. Regular eBay members can fix a Buy It Now price if they want to offer this facility as well.

Auctions normally run for 7 or 10 days, and it is important to think about the timing as it will end at the same time as the start. If selling in the UK only, you should make sure that people will be home from work when the last frantic minutes of bidding take place.

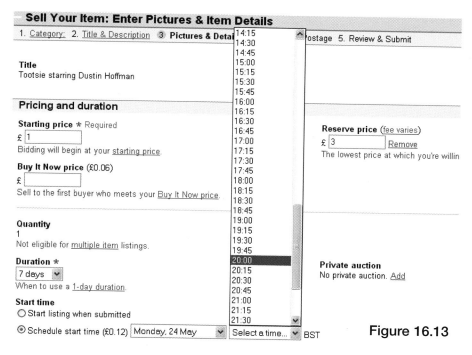

Figure 16.13

5. Most items on eBay need to be displayed visually to attract buyers, so take a picture of your object with a digital camera and add this to the page by clicking **Browse for Picture 1** and finding the file on your computer. Videos, records and DVDs, for example, would simply need a copy of the box cover or sleeve. For certain items, providing different views or close-ups will be important, so pay the few pence to add further pictures if necessary.

Add pictures & Gallery

■ **Basic eBay Picture**
  Let eBay host your pictures

Your own Web hosting
Enter your picture URL

To add pictures to your listing, click on the "Browse..." buttons below.

Basic Picture Services

Picture 1 (free)
[　　　　　　　　　　　] [Browse...]

Picture 2 (£0.12)
[　　　　　　　　　　　] [Browse...]

Picture 3 (£0.12)
[　　　　　　　　　　　] [Browse...]

Figure 16.14

6. Decide on the payment methods you will accept, bearing in
   mind that PayPal (see page 128) is the safest but there is a
   handling fee. Click the **Learn more** link if you want to register
   with PayPal at this stage (see Figure 16.15).

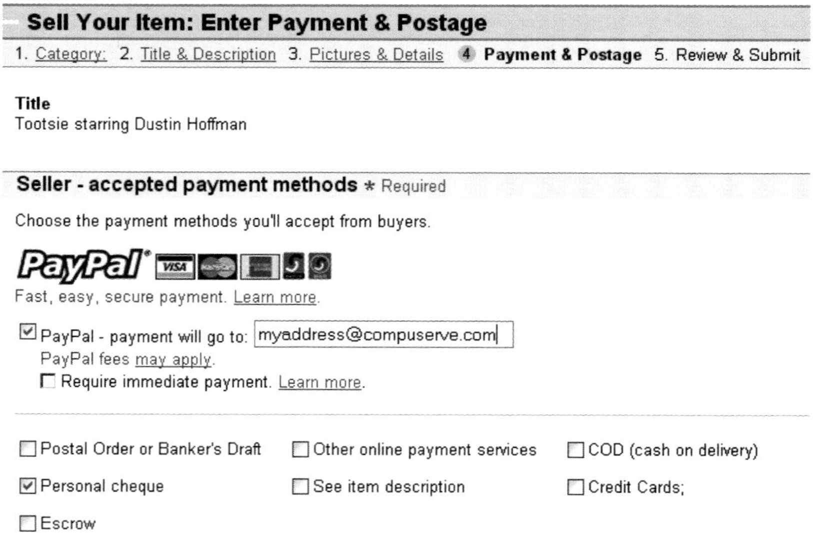

Sell Your Item: Enter Payment & Postage

1. Category: 2. Title & Description 3. Pictures & Details ④ **Payment & Postage** 5. Review & Submit

Title
Tootsie starring Dustin Hoffman

Seller - accepted payment methods * Required

Choose the payment methods you'll accept from buyers.

PayPal VISA 🔲 🔲 🔲 🔲 🔲
Fast, easy, secure payment. Learn more.

☑ PayPal - payment will go to: [myaddress@compuserve.com]
  PayPal fees may apply.
  ☐ Require immediate payment. Learn more.

☐ Postal Order or Banker's Draft   ☐ Other online payment services   ☐ COD (cash on delivery)

☑ Personal cheque   ☐ See item description   ☐ Credit Cards;

☐ Escrow

Figure 16.15

7. Now set the postage costs that your buyer must add, unless
   you are offering this as part of the deal or you want to discuss
   delivery with the buyer after the auction.

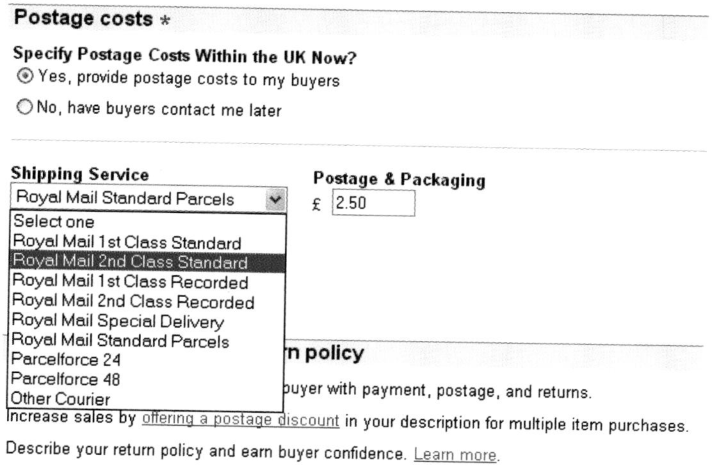

Postage costs *

Specify Postage Costs Within the UK Now?

⦿ Yes, provide postage costs to my buyers

○ No, have buyers contact me later

Shipping Service

Royal Mail Standard Parcels ▾

| Select one |
| Royal Mail 1st Class Standard |
| Royal Mail 2nd Class Standard |
| Royal Mail 1st Class Recorded |
| Royal Mail 2nd Class Recorded |
| Royal Mail Special Delivery |
| Royal Mail Standard Parcels |
| Parcelforce 24 |
| Parcelforce 48 |
| Other Courier |

Postage & Packaging

£ 2.50

n policy

buyer with payment, postage, and returns.

Increase sales by offering a postage discount in your description for multiple item purchases.

Describe your return policy and earn buyer confidence. Learn more.

Figure 16.16

8. The final screen will show you how much you must pay to advertise with eBay (which will be much cheaper than in a local newspaper) and the details that will be published on the Website. Check these carefully before clicking the final **Submit** button in case there are any errors or omissions, although you will be able to make some changes to your listing as long as the auction hasn't started and you haven't received any bids.

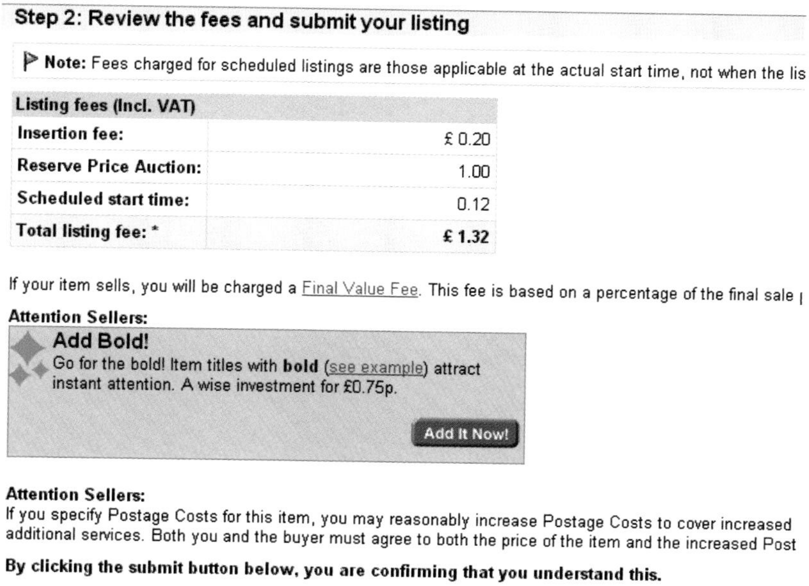

Step 2: Review the fees and submit your listing

▷ **Note:** Fees charged for scheduled listings are those applicable at the actual start time, not when the lis

Listing fees (Incl. VAT)

Insertion fee:	£ 0.20
Reserve Price Auction:	1.00
Scheduled start time:	0.12
Total listing fee: *	**£ 1.32**

If your item sells, you will be charged a Final Value Fee. This fee is based on a percentage of the final sale

Attention Sellers:

Add Bold!

Go for the bold! Item titles with **bold** (see example) attract instant attention. A wise investment for £0.75p.

Add It Now!

Attention Sellers:

If you specify Postage Costs for this item, you may reasonably increase Postage Costs to cover increased additional services. Both you and the buyer must agree to both the price of the item and the increased Post

Figure 16.17

By clicking the submit button below, you are confirming that you understand this.

9. You will probably find that bidding is very slow until the auction is in its last few hours, so go online regularly to check the price but don't give up hope until the auction has ended. During the 7 or 10 days, some eBay members may email you with various questions about your item – always reply promptly and in detail as you could otherwise endanger your sale.

17

Learning from a CD-ROM

A brief look at the shelves of many local shops will reveal a treasure trove of CD-ROMs that you can buy for as little as £4.99. They will teach you anything from how to type to making a will, using voice recognition software, designing a garden, selecting wine, finding the best pub or creating cartoons. They will also provide hours of entertainment in the form of computerised sports, fantasy, board or card games.

Figure 17.1

Before buying a CD-ROM, check the minimum requirements printed on the back of the case or in the accompanying booklet. You will be told the best version of your PC, the memory (RAM), sound card, processor speed and monitor settings that are necessary to run the program effectively. Don't be too worried if you have a reasonably modern machine and only want to run a simple program, but some of the advanced games may not run without the very latest sound and graphics cards.

To find out more about your machine, *right*-click the My Computer icon on the Desktop and select **Properties**. You will find the Windows version, RAM and processor speed of your machine (see Figure 17.2).

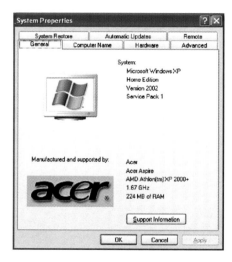

Figure 17.2

Project 22

Install and use a food encyclopaedia CD-ROM

Although you may have hundreds of recipe books, a food CD can be very helpful in planning meals. Not only can you create a quick list of many dishes that use the ingredients you happen to have in the fridge, you can also find out about their vitamin or mineral content and how to prepare unusual foods.

1. Insert the disk in your CD-ROM drive and wait for it to start automatically. If nothing happens after a few minutes, go to **Start – Run** and then click **Browse** (see Figure 17.3).

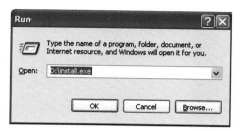

Figure 17.3

2. Locate the D:\ drive from the drop-down list in the **Look in:** box and then open the file labelled *Install* or *Setup*. A file ending **.exe** will appear in the Run box and you must click **OK** to start the process.

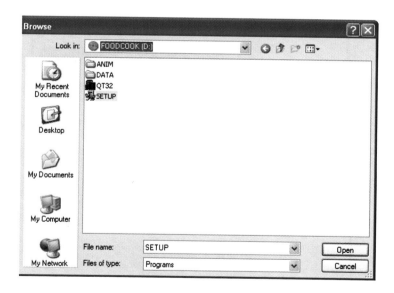

Figure 17.4

3. The first window for the installation process will appear and you can use the Wizard to install the program on your computer by clicking **Next** each time (see Figure 17.5). Unless you are sure you want to change these, accept the locations and names that are selected automatically.

Figure 17.5

4. The files needed to run the program will be copied onto your computer.

Figure 17.6

5. Whenever it appears, read and then click to accept the licence agreement (see Figure 17.7).

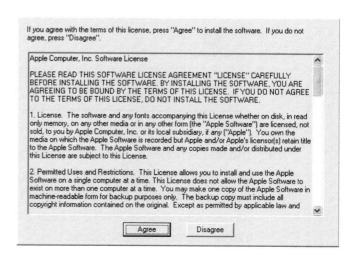

Figure 17.7

6. A new window may appear showing you the files being installed on your computer, and you will be told when the installation process is complete.

Figure 17.8

7. You may find that a window containing QuickTime icons will appear or you are told that QuickTime must be installed. This program is needed for viewing your CD-ROM images and the latest version will be installed if it is not detected on your machine.

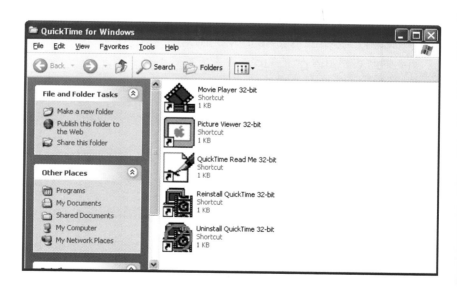

Figure 17.9

8. New programs sometimes include a shortcut that is placed on your Desktop. Double-click this shortcut to start your program. Otherwise, you can find it from the **Start – All Programs** menu. It may be under a general menu heading, and you will need to click the correct icon to launch the program.

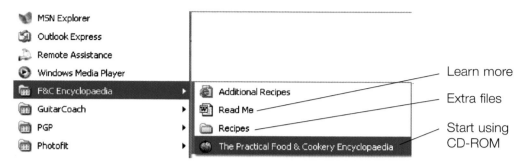

Learn more

Extra files

Start using
CD-ROM

Figure 17.10

9. In most cases, not all the files will be installed on your machine as they would take up too much space. You will therefore need to keep the CD-ROM in the drive when using the program.

10. For each program, there will be indexes, menus and toolbars to learn how to use. Some CD-ROMs are very well designed and seem straightforward, but in many cases it may take a while to understand the system. Resting the mouse pointer on parts of the screen should reveal tips and definitions, but, if it is too confusing, consult the *Read Me* file which will have been installed with the program.

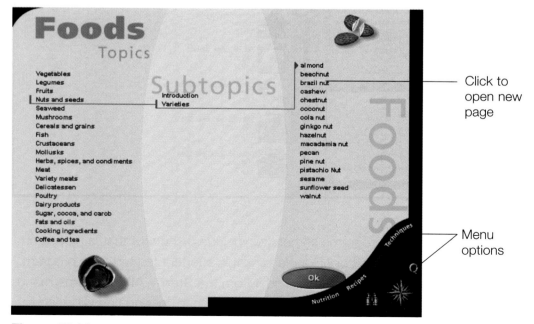

Click to
open new
page

Menu
options

Figure 17.11

11. At some stage, you may decide you no longer want the program taking up space on your computer. Don't try to delete individual files, as you may remove shared files that are needed by other programs. Instead, locate the program folder from the **Start – All Programs** menu and select the **Uninstall** option (see Figure 17.12).

Figure 17.12

Remove from computer

12. If this option is not available, open **Start – Control Panel** and select **Add or Remove Programs**. Locate the program in the list, select it and click **Change/Remove** (see Figure 17.13). All the files will be fully removed.

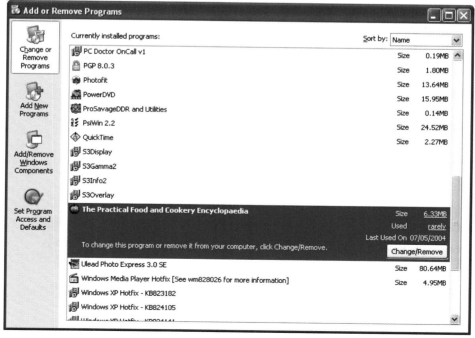

Figure 17.13

Customising your Desktop

If you use your computer a fair amount of time each week, you may want to change the way it has been set up, to make it easier or more enjoyable to use. This is known as 'customising'.

Shortcuts

When you first buy a computer, a few shortcuts will have been added to your Desktop. These often include a link to your Internet browser, email system, the computer itself (My Computer), and the My Documents folder where you save your work. For anyone using Microsoft Office programs, it is also common to install the shortcut toolbar which can be positioned along the top or side of the screen.

If you want to add it, insert the Office XP disk and then go to **Start – Control Panel – Add or Remove Programs**. Find your Microsoft Office program listed in the contents that will appear, select it in the list and click **Change**. Select the **Add or Remove Features** option and then click on **Office Tools**. You will see one item is the Shortcut bar. Click the arrow in the button on the left and select **Run from My Computer**. Click **Update** and it will be installed.

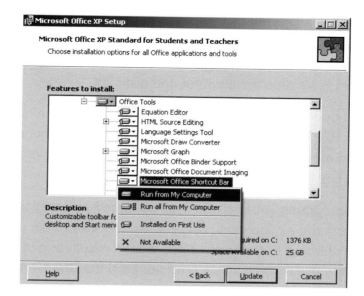

Figure 18.1

If you want to change the shortcuts that are available on the toolbar, click the blue area at the top and select **Customize – Buttons**. You can now click to add a tick in any box next to a program you use often, or click *off* unwanted buttons that are taking up space. To add other shortcuts, for example to an actual file or folder containing commonly used files, click the appropriate **Add File** or **Add Folder** button and find the target files within your computer.

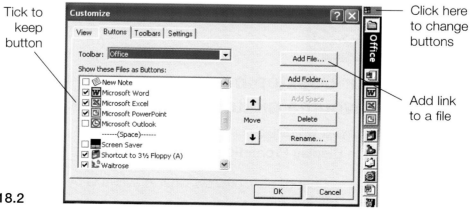

Figure 18.2

To add shortcuts to the Desktop area, *right*-click any part of the screen and select **New – Shortcut**. You will be asked to browse through your computer files until you see the target program and can select it, rename the shortcut and click **OK**.

When it appears, it will display a small arrow showing it is a shortcut.  Deleting such icons if you change your mind will *not* affect the actual files or programs: it will only remove the Desktop link to them.

Links to programs you use often will be added automatically to the **Start** menu as you work, and you can choose to *pin* a program shortcut to the menu if you want it readily available. You can do this if you find the program from the **Start – All Programs** list. *Right*-click the name and then click the option **Pin to Start menu** (see Figure 18.3).

Add link

Figure 18.3

Project 23

Change your Desktop background to display a favourite picture

Windows XP machines will display one of a range of pictures provided within the **Display Properties** dialog box.

1. To change your current display, preview what is available by opening the box in one of two ways:

a. Go to **Start** – **Control Panel**, double-click **Display** and click the **Desktop** tab (see Figure 18.4);

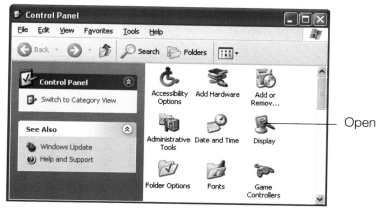

Figure 18.4

or

b. *right*-click on any part of the Desktop and select **Properties** – **Desktop**.

2. Click any picture in the **Background**: list to see it in the preview window. To see the effect on the Desktop, click **Apply**. Having found a picture you prefer, make the change permanent by clicking **OK**.

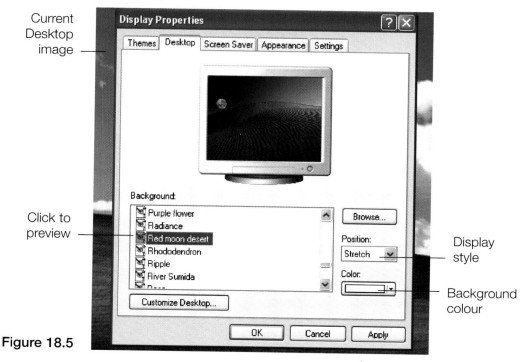

Figure 18.5

3. There are three different ways the actual picture can be displayed:

- *Tiled* (a number of small pictures arranged across the screen);
- *Centred* (the picture will reveal a plain or patterned surround, chosen from the colour options); or
- *Stretched* (it will fill the screen but may be distorted).

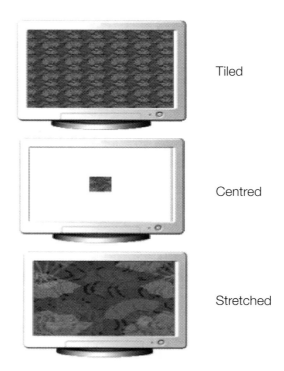

Tiled

Centred

Stretched

Figure 18.6

4. To display your own choice of picture, click the **Browse** button in the Display window and locate the file in the normal way. Select the one you want on your Desktop and click **Open**.

Figure 18.7

Click to select picture

5. It will reappear in the preview window, and its name will be added to the list of background pictures. Select an appropriate style and, if centred, an alternative surround colour and then click **OK**.

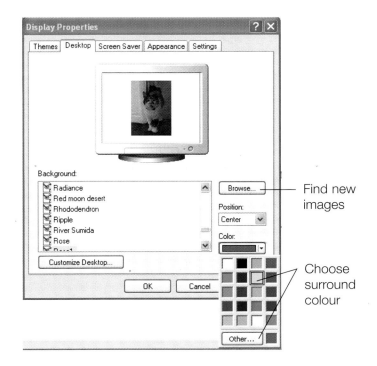

Find new images

Choose surround colour

Figure 18.8

6. After a short wait, you will find your new picture and colour scheme will now be displayed on the Desktop.

Figure 18.9

Using spreadsheets

Spreadsheet programs such as Microsoft Excel are excellent for working out complicated sums and playing around with the numbers to see how they affect the results. This is because they perform calculations based on instructions you give them in the form of 'formulae'. As long as the formulae contain a reference to the contents of particular cells in a spreadsheet, and not the actual figures, whenever these change the calculations are updated automatically.

Formulae

When you open Excel, you see a vast grid of squares (known as 'cells'). Any letters or numbers that you type will automatically appear in the cell that shows a black border. This is the 'active cell' and you can click any cell, or press Enter or the tab key, to activate a different cell.

Cells are known by the letter at the top of their column and the number of their row. So cell A4 is in column A and row 4.

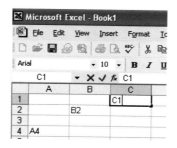

Figure 19.1

To perform a calculation on numbers typed in various cells, for example to add the numbers typed below, click the cell where you want the answer to appear and then type an = symbol. Excel recognises this as an instruction to perform a calculation.

Figure 19.2

- To add numbers, use the + operator
- To subtract numbers, use the – operator
- To multiply numbers, use the * operator
- To divide numbers, use the / operator

To add the numbers in cells A1, A2 and A3, you would click cell A4 and then type:

$$=A1+A2+A3$$

The answer will appear in the cell when you press Enter, and the formula in any selected cell will be visible in the bar across the top of the sheet known as the Formula Bar.

Result in cell

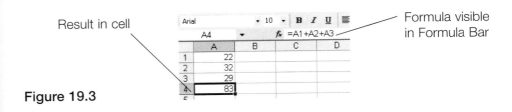

Formula visible in Formula Bar

Figure 19.3

Do *not* type = 22+32+29 as you would have to edit the formula whenever the numbers were changed.

In the same way, to multiply the figure in cell B2 by 20, you would click the cell where you want the answer to appear (cell C2 in Figure 19.4) and type:

$$=B2*20$$

	A	B	C	D
	C2		f_x =B2*20	
1	TOOLS	PRICE	TOTAL SALES	
2	Fork	43.25	865	
3	Wheelbarrow	85.99		
4	Spade	39		
5	Hoe	28.5		

Figure 19.4

Totals

To add up a long column or row of figures, it is quicker to use the automatic tool – the **AutoSum** Σ . Select the full range of cells by dragging across them with the pointer when it shows a white cross ⊕ . Now click the **AutoSum** button to add the total to the next empty cell.

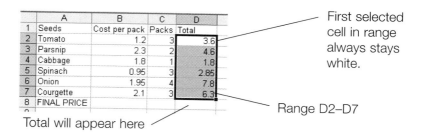

	A	B	C	D
1	Seeds	Cost per pack	Packs	Total
2	Tomato	1.2	3	3.6
3	Parsnip	2.3	2	4.6
4	Cabbage	1.8	1	1.8
5	Spinach	0.95	3	2.85
6	Onion	1.95	4	7.8
7	Courgette	2.1	3	6.3
8	FINAL PRICE			

First selected cell in range always stays white.

Range D2–D7

Figure 19.5   Total will appear here

Formatting cell contents

After typing letters or numbers into a spreadsheet, you can change their appearance by selecting them and using the toolbar.

Change font type and size, and format entries to **bold**, *italic* or <u>underlined</u> using the toolbar buttons.   Arial   ▾ 10 ▾ **B** *I* <u>U</u>

	A	B	C	D
1	**Seeds**	**Cost per pack**	**Packs**	**Total**
2	Tomato	1.2	3	3.6
3	Parsnip	2.3	2	4.6
4	Cabbage	1.8	1	1.8
5	Spinach	0.95	3	2.85
6	Onion	1.95	4	7.8
7	Courgette	2.1	3	6.3
8	FINAL PRICE			26.95
9				

Figure 19.6

For numbers, it is best to open the **Format – Cells** menu and
click the **Number** tab. Select the number category – for example
currency, percentage, date or number – and, where relevant, set
the correct number of decimals or add a symbol or separator.
Check the preview before clicking **OK** (see Figure 19.7).

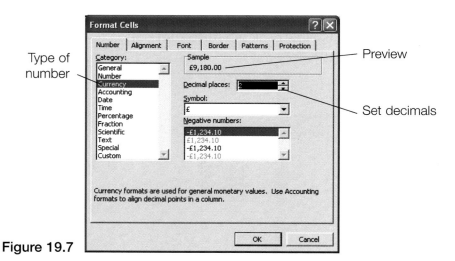

Type of
number

Preview

Set decimals

Figure 19.7

Saving

Spreadsheet files are known as 'Workbooks' and are saved in
the same way as word-processed documents. The equivalent of
a page is a worksheet, and Workbooks can have as many as
you like – just add them from the **Insert** menu. Worksheets are
saved automatically when you save the file.

Project 24

Work out your BMI (Body Mass Index) to monitor weight loss

Nowadays, dieters don't rely so much on their exact weight. Instead, a better indication of a healthy weight is provided by the Body Mass Index (BMI). BMI is worked out using a complicated formula related to your weight and height, and the ideal is to be between 20 and 25. The international classification for BMI is:

Below 20: underweight

20 – 25: acceptable weight

25 – 30: overweight

30 – 40: obese

Over 40: very obese

The calculation involves dividing your weight in kilograms by your squared height in metres. As many of us still rely on stones, pounds, feet and inches, this makes the calculation even more complicated.

A computer spreadsheet is an excellent way to keep track of your BMI. As you lose weight, simply enter the new figures into the spreadsheet: the calculation will automatically update to take these into account.

1. Open a new Workbook in Excel and enter the headings shown in Figure 19.8 in the cells. Format the entries – for example to be bold or underlined – if that makes the spreadsheet clearer.

Figure 19.8

	A	B	C
1	WEIGHT		
2	Stone	Lbs	Weight in lbs
3			

2. If you cannot see an entry clearly, widen the column. Do this by moving the mouse pointer to the line between letters at the top of the columns and dragging the border to the right when the

pointer shows a two-way arrow (see Figure 19.9). You can also double-click this line to adjust the column width to fit the longest entry exactly.

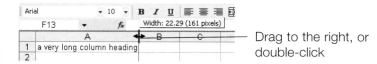

Figure 19.9

Drag to the right, or double-click

3. Type in figures for your weight in cells A3 and B3; for example 9st 13lbs. To work out your weight in lbs, you need to multiply the 9st by 14 and then add the extra lbs. The formula in cell C3 is therefore

$$=A3*14+B3$$

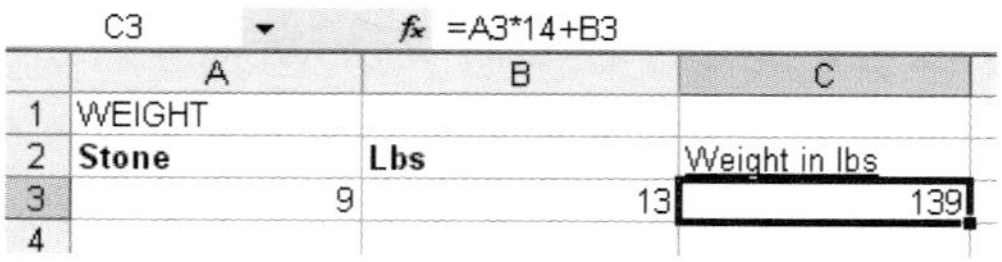

Figure 19.10

4. For the BMI calculation you must express your current weight in kilograms. This means dividing the pounds displayed in C3 by 2.2. Add a new heading *Weight in kilograms* in cell B5 and type the correct formula in cell C5.

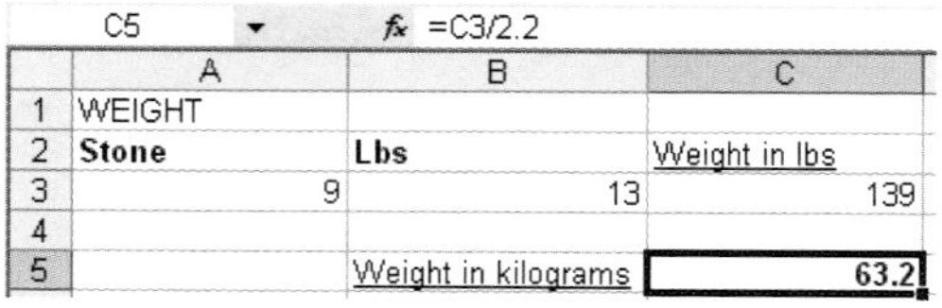

Figure 19.11

5. Now you need your height in metres: add headings for feet and inches and type in your height; for example 5ft 5ins. Enter a formula to work out the height in inches (multiply the ft by 12 and add the extra inches).

	A	B	C
	C8 ▼		fx =A8*12+B8
1	WEIGHT		
2	Stone	Lbs	Weight in lbs
3		9	13	139
4			
5		Weight in kilograms	63.2
6	HEIGHT		
7	Ft	Inches	Height in inches
8		5	5	65
9			

Figure 19.12

6. To express inches in metres, you must multiply the figure by 0.025, so enter the correct formula in cell C10.

	A	B	C
	C10 ▼		fx =C8*0.025
1	WEIGHT		
2	Stone	Lbs	Weight in lbs
3		9	13	139
4			
5		Weight in kilograms	63.2
6	HEIGHT		
7	Ft	Inches	Height in inches
8		5	5	65
9			
10		Height in Metres	1.6

Figure 19.13

7. To work out the BMI in cell B13, you must square the height measurement (see cell C11) and then divide your weight in kilograms by the squared height in metres. The final spreadsheet will contain these formulae:

	A	B	C
1	WEIGHT		
2	Stone	Lbs	Weight in lbs
3	9	13	=A3*14+B3
4			
5		Weight in kilograms	=C3/2.2
6	HEIGHT		
7	Ft	Inches	Height in inches
8	5	5	=A8*12+B8
9			
10		Height in Metres	=C8*0.025
11		Squared metres	=C10*C10
12			
13	BMI	=C5/C11	
14			

Figure 19.14

8. The actual BMI in this case is 24 (see Figure 19.15). As you lose weight, change the entries in cells A3 and B3 and the final BMI will be updated automatically.

	A	B	C
1	WEIGHT		
2	Stone	Lbs	Weight in lbs
3	9	13	139
4			
5		Weight in kilograms	63.2
6	HEIGHT		
7	Ft	Inches	Height in inches
8	5	5	65
9			
10		Height in Metres	1.6
11		Squared metres	2.6
12			
13	BMI	24	

Figure 19.15

9. Keep your spreadsheet safe by clicking the **Save** button and changing the file name from *Book1* to *BMI*.

Project 25

Create and search a family database

As well as performing calculations, spreadsheet programs are very useful for building up databases of information about people or objects, such as record or book collections. One useful database might include friends or members of your family, where you could keep any useful details, such as dress size, birthdays, favourite food, phone numbers or allergies, etc.

1. To create a family database, decide on the main categories under which the information will be stored and set these out as column headings. It is always a good idea to include *more* rather than fewer headings, in case you need to search for people in a different way. For example, a single column including everyone's full name isn't as useful as two columns holding first names and surnames separately.

A	B	C	D	E	F	G	H	I	J
My Family									
First name	Surname	Relationship	Age	Birthday	Address1	Address 2	Town	Postcode	Telephone

Figure 19.16

2. If you realise you have forgotten a category, click the column heading letter to the *right* and go to **Insert – Columns**. A new column will 'slide' into place and you can type in the new heading.

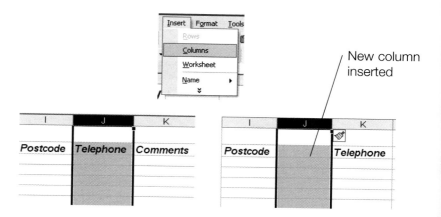

Figure 19.17

3. Start entering everyone's details into your database. You will find that, if you repeat a letter at the beginning of an entry, you may automatically be offered the earlier entry in full. Either press your tab or Enter key to accept it or keep typing and override the suggestion.

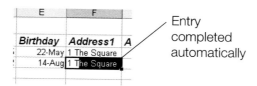

Figure 19.18

4. Once you have typed some of the details, save the database to keep the information safe. A complete entry for any one person is known as a 'record'. You can add a huge number of records, as each spreadsheet contains thousands of rows.

5. One important aspect of a database is to format the numerical data properly. As long as the program recognises dates and numbers, it can perform calculations and find dates beginning before, after or between those specified, or numbers that are larger or smaller.

6. Any numbers will be placed on the right in a cell, with text appearing on the left. To change the appearance of numerical data but not the underlying values, select all the entries in any column and then go to **Format – Cells – Number**. Choose **Currency** or **Date**, etc, from the **Category:** list and then set decimal places or number/date style.

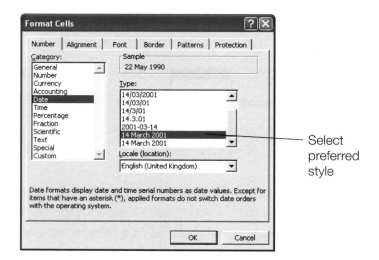

Select preferred style

Figure 19.19

7. Having completed all your entries, you are ready to use the database to carry out a search. For example, if you want to see the records for all your brothers, or find if any of your relatives are under 20, select all the main data and open the **Data** menu. Click **Filter – AutoFilter** (see Figure 19.20).

Surname	Relationship	Age	Birthday		Address1	Address 2	Town	P
Williams	Niece	14	22 September 1990	1 The Square			Bingwell	BC
Williams	Nephew	12	14 August 1992	1 The Square			Bingwell	BC
Wiliams	Sister	44	01 December 1960	1 The Square			Bingwell	BC
Binns	Brother	54	02 January 1950	34 Western Road	Sotwell		Birmingha	BI
Binns	Brother	62	12 March 1942	The Almshouse	5 Winton Drive	Kingston	TS
Sweeney	Sister	44	03 September 1960	5 Peters Court	Minder Close	Brighton	BN
Sweeney	Brother in law	45	11 November 1959	5 Peters Court	Minder Close	Brighton	BN

Figure 19.20

8. Arrows will appear next to each heading. Click one to display all the entries for that category. For a simple search of matching entries, click one entry – only records that match will be displayed.

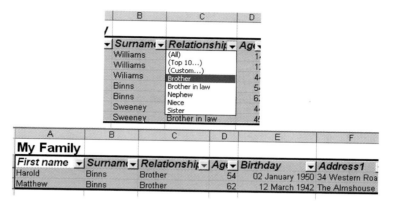

Figure 19.21

9. Before carrying out a new search, click **(All)** in the category you have previously searched to show all the records again or select the **Show All** option from the **Data – Filter** menu. In some cases, you may prefer to carry out a second search based on this subset of your database to refine the search further.

10. For searching that relies on a calculation or logical statement rather than an exact match, click the **(Custom)** entry for any category; for example in the *Age* column. You can now set the criteria for searching for teenagers. Choose from the drop-down menus and, if necessary, type your own figures in the boxes.

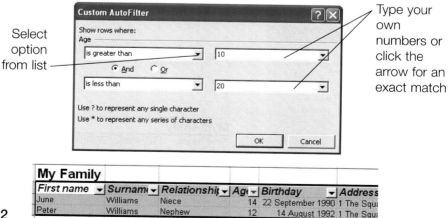

Figure 19.22

11. To find records where an entry is not known in full, choose **begins with** or **contains** or use the * for the unknown characters.

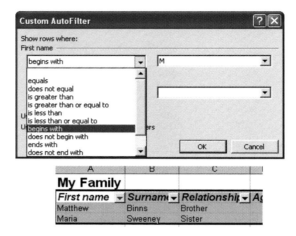

Figure 19.23

12. A final function that may make your database more useful is to reorder (sort) all the records; for example by town, surname or age. Take off the filter mechanism by selecting **Data** – **Filter** and clicking **AutoFilter** to remove the tick, but keep the data selected. Now you can select the **Sort** option from the same menu.

13. Decide on the order of your sort – for example first by *Surname* and then by *First Name* – and make these selections from the boxes. Check that you are sorting in the correct order – alphabetical, from lowest to highest is **Ascending**, and from highest to lowest is **Descending** – and then click **OK**.

Figure 19.24

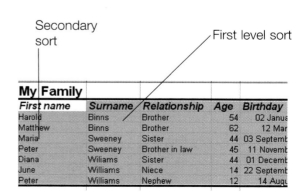

About Age Concern

Age Concern is the UK's largest organisation working for and with older people to enable them to make more of life. We are a federation of over 400 independent charities which share the same name, values and standards.

We believe that ageing is a normal part of life, and that later life should be fulfilling, enjoyable and productive. We enable older people by providing services and grants, researching their needs and opinions, influencing government and media, and through other innovative and dynamic projects.

Every day we provide vital services, information and support to thousands of older people of all ages and backgrounds.

Age Concern also works with many older people from disadvantaged or marginalised groups, such as those living in rural areas or black and minority ethnic elders.

Age Concern is dependent on donations, covenants and legacies.

Age Concern England
1268 London Road
London SW16 4ER
Tel: 020 8765 7200
Fax: 020 8765 7211
Website:
www.ageconcern.org.uk

Age Concern Scotland
113 Rose Street
Edinburgh EH2 3DT
Tel: 0131 220 3345
Fax: 0131 220 2779
Website:
www.ageconcernscotland.org.uk

Age Concern Cymru
Ty John Pathy
Units 13 and 14
Neptune Court
Vanguard Way
Cardiff CF24 5PJ
Tel: 029 2043 1555
Website:
www.accymru.org.uk

Age Concern Northern Ireland
3 Lower Crescent
Belfast BT7 1NR
Tel: 028 9024 5729
Fax: 028 9023 5497
Website:
www.ageconcernni.org

Publications from Age Concern Books

Age Concern Books publishes over 65 books, training packs and learning resources aimed at older people, their families, friends and carers, as well as professionals working with and for older people. Publications include:

Getting the Most from your Computer

A practical guide for older home users: 2nd edition

Jackie Sherman

Older people who are computer literate are in the enviable position of being able to control their lives – staying in touch with family and friends, arranging holidays and leisure activities, ordering food or goods to be delivered at home, and much more. This book is an invaluable guide for anybody who is interested in computers and who wishes to advance their knowledge and skills.

It ranges from the basics of buying and setting up a system appropriate to the person's financial situation, plus an introduction to all the commonly-used packages such as *Word*, *Excel* and *PowerPoint*, to more advanced topics, so that readers can learn how to produce animated presentations, run their own budget on a spreadsheet or use the desktop publishing features of a word-processing package. There is also a large section on sending and organising emails and getting the most out of the World Wide Web.

£7.99 0-86242-392-9

How to be a Silver Surfer

A beginner's guide to the Internet: 2nd edition

Emma Aldridge

This revised and updated bestselling guide contains new chapters on using the Internet for shopping, banking, family trees and gardening. It is a companion guide for people who are new to the Internet and a little apprehensive about what to do. Using simple step-by-step explanations, it will 'hand-hold' readers through the most important tasks when first using the Internet. Topics include searching the Web, sending an email and saving a favourite Web page for future reference.

Aimed at people over 50, the emphasis is on using the Internet as a tool to enrich existing interests, such as travel, fishing, aromatherapy, cooking and furniture restoration, and as a recreational activity in itself – for example playing online bridge, emailing family and friends, and using chat sites. It can also ensure you don't miss out on good deals and last-minute bargains.

£5.99 0-86242-379-1

Changing Direction

Employment options in working life: 2nd edition

Sue Ward

Changing direction later rather than earlier in working life can be challenging – and enforced change (perhaps early retirement or redundancy) can be worrying – but it can also provide an opportunity for a new beginning in a possibly more satisfying second career. This revised and updated edition will help you to identify and find outlets for your skills, whether as an employee, a self-employed person, or a volunteer. It guides you through the many steps which can be taken, including:

- deciding what you really want to do
- retraining and educational opportunities
- looking for work (employed and self-employed)
- help from the state
- sorting out your financial position
- combating age discrimination
- voluntary work.

£9.99 0-86242-331-7

Your Guide to Retirement

Ro Lyon

This bestselling book encourages everyone to view retirement as an opportunity. It is full of useful suggestions and information on:

- managing money: pensions, tax, savings, wills
- making the most of your time: learning and leisure, earning money
- your home: moving, repairing, security, raising income
- staying healthy: looking after yourself, help with health costs
- relationships: sexuality, bereavement, caring for someone.

It is an invaluable guide for people coming up to retirement, planning ahead for retirement, or newly retired, as well as for employers and welfare advisers.

£7.99 0-86242-350-3

Your Rights

A guide to money benefits for older people

Sally West

Your Rights has established itself as *the* money benefits guide for older people. Updated annually, and written in clear, jargon-free language, it ensures that older people – and their advisers – can easily understand the complexities of state benefits and discover the full range of financial support available to them.

£5.99: For more information, please telephone 0870 44 22 120.

To order from Age Concern Books

Call our **hotline: 0870 44 22 120** (for orders or a free books catalogue)

Opening hours 9am–7pm Monday to Friday, 10am–5pm Saturday and Sunday

Books can also be ordered from our secure online bookshop: **www.ageconcern.org.uk/shop**

Alternatively, you can write to Age Concern Books, Units 5 and 6 Industrial Estate, Brecon, Powys LD3 8LA. Fax: 0870 8000 100. Please enclose a cheque or money order for the appropriate amount plus p&p made payable to Age Concern England. Credit card orders can be made on the order hotline.

Our **postage and packing** costs are as follows: mainland UK and Northern Ireland: £1.99 for the first book, 75p for each additional book up to a maximum of £7.50. For customers ordering from outside the mainland UK and NI: credit card payment only; please telephone for international postage rates or email sales@ageconcernbooks.co.uk

Bulk order discounts

Age Concern Books is pleased to offer a discount on orders totalling 50 or more copies of the same title. For details, please contact Age Concern Books on 0870 44 22 120.

Customised editions

Age Concern Books is pleased to offer a free 'customisation' service for anyone wishing to purchase 500 or more copies of most titles. This gives you the option to have a unique front cover design featuring your organisation's logo and corporate colours, or adding your logo to the current cover design. You can also insert an additional four pages of text for a small additional fee. Existing clients include many prominent names in British industry, retailing and finance, the trade union movement, educational establishments, private and voluntary sectors, and welfare associations. For full details, please contact Sue Henning, Age Concern Books, Astral House, 1268 London Road, London SW16 4ER. Fax: 020 8765 7211. Email: hennins@ace.org.uk

Age Concern Information Line/Factsheets subscription

Age Concern produces more than 45 comprehensive factsheets designed to answer many of the questions older people (or those advising them) may have. These include money and benefits, health, community care, leisure and education, and housing. For up to five free factsheets, telephone 0800 00 99 66 (8am–7pm, seven days a week, every week of the year). Alternatively, you may prefer to write to Age Concern, FREEPOST (SWB 30375), ASHBURTON, Devon TQ13 7ZZ.

For professionals working with older people, the factsheets are available on an annual subscription service, which includes updates throughout the year. For further details and costs of the subscription, please contact Age Concern at the above Freepost address.

Glossary

Accessing Finding and opening a Web page.

Active cell The cell showing a black border, in which any data will appear when you type text or numbers. You **activate** a new cell by clicking in it with the mouse or moving there by pressing the Tab, Enter or arrow keys.

Active window When more than one window is open at the same time, this is the only window with a blue title bar in which you are able to work.

Application The named software that is dedicated to a related group of tasks, such as word processing or drawing (eg Word or Publisher).

Bitmap file A graphics (picture) file created when using an application such as Microsoft Paint and made up of a collection of coloured dots known as pixels.

Bookmarking Storing a favourite Web page address so that it can be opened again easily.

Browsing (see Surfing)

Browser The application that allows you to view Web pages on the World Wide Web.

CD-ROMs Shiny round disks placed on the slide-out tray in your computer that contain applications, such as encyclopaedias, games, drawing packages or music.

Cells Squares in tables or spreadsheets where you enter your data.

Central Processing Unit (CPU) The heart of your computer that controls its main functions.

Chat rooms A special kind of Website where you can communicate in writing with other people online at the same time.

Glossary

Clicking Pressing a button on your mouse to instruct the computer to carry out a particular task.

Clipboard An area of the computer memory where you temporarily store text or images before moving or copying them to another file or within the same file.

Compressing files (see Zipping)

Cursor A flashing black bar that marks the text insertion point.

Database Information about people or things stored in a systematic way that can be sorted or searched.

Default Settings for your work or the equipment you are using that are selected automatically and can be accepted or changed manually.

Desktop The opening screen you see when you turn on your computer. Its name derives from the various little pictures you see that represent items in an office, such as a wastepaper basket (the Recycle Bin).

Dialog box Small windows (opened via a menu) that offer you various choices to click or type in.

Digital camera Equipment that creates digital pictures that can be viewed and stored on the computer.

Domain name Parts of a Web address that display an organisation's registered name, location and type of business.

Double-clicking Clicking the left mouse button twice very fast. It is used as a quick method to open programs or files and can be replaced by selecting the item with one click of the left mouse button and then pressing the Enter key on the keyboard.

Downloading Transferring files from the Internet onto your own computer.

Drive Slot in the computer housing a disk and usually referred to by letter; for example, the C: drive (for the hard disk) or A: drive (for a floppy disk).

Driver Software program needed to operate hardware such as printers, modems, graphics cards, scanners and cameras.

Email Electronic messages sent via the Internet.

Fieldname The heading or category under which information in a database is stored.

File Piece of work – text, numbers, images or other objects – created and saved onto a computer.

File type/extension Parts of a file name showing in which application it has been produced or what type of file it is.

Floppy disk 3½" squares of plastic on which files can be stored. They can be carried around so that files can be reopened on different machines.

Folder Labelled space where you can store related programs and files.

Font Type of character used when typing text or numbers.

Formula Instructions to the computer to carry out a calculation.

Function Instructions recognised by a spreadsheet application to perform specific calculations.

Function keys Keys along the top of the keyboard that do not relate to any characters but act as shortcuts to various actions; for example, opening the Help menu (F1) or checking spelling (F7).

Gateway Website that can be searched for links to other sites on a single theme (eg education, health, etc).

Greyscale View of a picture that shows shades of grey instead of colours.

Hard disk Main area within the computer on which programs and files are stored.

Hardware Parts of the computer you can see and touch.

Help Demonstrations, explanations and other assistance available when working on your computer.

Hyperlink Text or pictures that are embedded in Web pages and can be clicked to open related pages.

Icons Small pictures representing programs or shortcuts to common tasks.

Glossary

Internet Computers around the world that are linked and can share information.

ISP (Internet Service Provider) The organisation that supplies software and facilities to allow you to link to the Internet and send emails.

IT (Information Technology) The technical term for using technology to communicate and handle information.

Jpeg file A type of graphics file that is recognised by a browser so that pictures (often photographs) can be displayed on the Web. The other common Web graphics file format is a gif file.

Justify Text is spread across the page to 'neaten' its appearance on the right-hand margin.

Keywords Any important words or phrases typed into a query/search box that form the basis of a search for relevant records or Websites.

Log in Entering your personal name and password to access secure areas on a computer.

Marquee Dotted lines showing a selected area.

Megapixels (see Resolution)

Modem The hardware required to allow digital computer information to travel down standard telephone lines.

Mouse Hardware that allows you to move a pointer on screen and click a button to instruct the computer to carry out a particular task.

Newsgroups Groups of people with a common interest who communicate via email.

Online/offline Connected or disconnected from the Internet.

Operating system Software controlling the general operation of the computer.

Optical Character Recognition (OCR) The technology that allows typewritten material to be scanned into a computer in the form of a word-processed document.

Orientation The setting you select that determines how a page is printed – either upright (Portrait), or turned sideways (Landscape) so that the longer sides are top and bottom.

Package (see Application)

PC (Personal Computer) The type of computer that sits on your desk at home or work and contains most of the programs and files you use.

Placeholder An area already in place on a slide where you can insert different objects, such as charts or pictures.

Programs Ordered sets of instructions that the computer carries out.

RAM (Random Access Memory) The memory your computer uses to open and run the different applications.

Relational database An application that allows you to search for related data across a number of tables of information.

Resolution The sharpness of a picture. Resolution is measured in millions of pixels ('dots') known as megapixels.

Scanner Equipment used to transfer text or images from paper onto computer.

Search engine A Website that holds a vast database of Web pages that you search using keywords.

Server A remote computer in a networked system that houses the network operating system software along with any software applications and data files that need to be shared.

Shareware Programs or files on the World Wide Web that are either free or very cheap to use.

Shortcut A way of carrying out common tasks without needing to go through the menu options. Common shortcuts are available within each application by clicking toolbar buttons at the top of the screen.

Software The instructions, in the form of programs, that the computer needs to be able to work effectively.

Spam Unsolicited emails – same as 'junk mail'.

Spreadsheet Text labels and numerical data created using a program that can perform calculations.

Surfing (or browsing) Describes the activity of searching the Internet for information.

Task Pane An optional sidebar that appears within Office XP applications offering shortcuts to related activities.

Taskbar The blue bar along the bottom of the screen that is always available and which houses the *Start* button, some general information such as the time and date, any minimised files and shortcuts to some of your applications or controls.

Template A file that is used to create a variety of different files based on its contents and style but that is left unaltered.

TFT The technology used to create computer monitor screens that are thin and flat and take up far less room than normal desktop monitors.

Toolbar Rows of buttons that act as shortcuts to the more common activities carried out when using your computer. Each toolbar contains a set of buttons related to a particular group of tasks, such as *Drawing* or *Tables*.

URL (Uniform Resource Locator) The address of any Web page.

Username Your identifying name for logging in, or as part of your email address.

Virus Rogue programs that damage your files and are 'caught' via the Internet or from infected floppy disks.

Web page Documents containing text, pictures, sounds, moving images etc, written in code (usually HTML), that are stored on computers around the world and can be viewed when you connect to the Internet.

Website A collection of linked Web pages found at the same address and created by a single organisation.

Wizards Guides found in various Microsoft applications that can help you produce files or objects step-by-step.

Workbook The name given to files created in Excel. Each Workbook contains a number of sheets that are saved with the file.

World Wide Web (known as **the Web** or **WWW**) All the multimedia Web pages displayed in a browser window when you connect to the Internet.

Zipping Reducing the size of files so that they take up less room and can be sent more easily by email or stored on disk.

Appendix: Basic computing

The Desktop

When you turn on your computer, after a few moments you will see your opening screen. This is the Desktop. It will have a coloured background and will display the following basic items:

Icons: small pictures will represent some parts of your computer, such as:

- *the Recycle Bin*, where unwanted items are stored until removed completely;
- *My Documents*, which is a folder in which you can store your work; and
- *My Computer*, which provides access to everything in your machine.

Taskbar: this is the blue bar running across the bottom of the screen. It is available wherever you are in your computer. It contains the green **Start** button that provides access to all your programs, and may also display different icons depending on how your machine has been set up. For example, Figure A1 below shows an icon for anti-virus checking software and a red cross next to a double computer symbol which means that the computer is not connected to the Internet. The current time is also visible.

Clicking the **Start** button opens the **Start** menu from which you can search for missing work, receive help on using your computer, open My Computer if it is not visible on the Desktop, change many of the computer settings, or connect to the Internet.

If you have purchased Microsoft Office software, you may also see a shortcut to the various programs it contains. It will be in the form

Background ——

Recycle Bin icon ——

Start button

Figure A1

Office shortcut bar

Shows that the computer is not connected to the Internet

Anti-virus checking software icon

Taskbar

of the Office Shortcut Bar running down the side of your screen or across the top.

Mouse

Most people are familiar with a keyboard, but mastering the mouse (the main method for giving instructions to the machine) can take a while. As you drag the mouse gently across the desk, it will move an arrow on the screen. This is the pointer.

To select – position the pointer over any object and press down the *left* mouse button briefly before letting go. This is known as 'clicking'. If you click an icon on the Desktop, it will change colour. If you click a menu, a list of options will appear, and if you click in a box you will confirm an action such as closing or deleting.

To open – you can use the mouse to open an icon if you click the *left* mouse button twice, very fast. This is 'double-clicking'. An alternative is to select the object with one click and then press the Enter key on the keyboard.

To move/drag – position the pointer over an object, press down the *left* button and keep it held down as you drag the mouse across the screen.

Shortcut menu – if you click the *right* mouse button on any part of the screen, you will open a short menu of relevant options. To choose one, click it once with the *left* mouse button. The chosen option will usually change colour.

Menu
produced by
right-clicking —

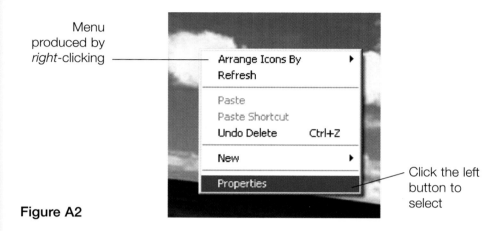

Click the left
button to
select

Figure A2

Windows

Each object on the Desktop, and all the programs you will be using, can be opened up. They will appear inside a window and, although each program will have its own special tools, the basic structure and management of these windows is very similar.

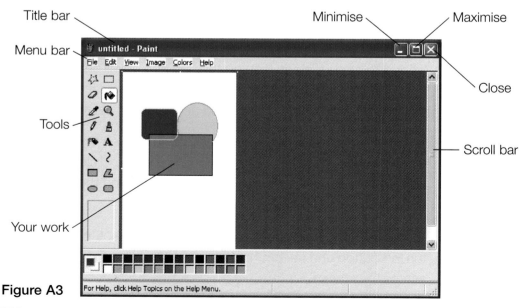

Title bar

Menu bar

Minimise

Maximise

Close

Tools

Scroll bar

Your work

Figure A3

Title bar – this shows the program you are using and the name of the piece of work. It will be untitled until your work is saved (see Chapter 1).

Minimise button – click this to keep your work open but out of the way – it will be 'parked' on the taskbar and can be restored with one click.

Maximise button – click this to expand the window to fill the entire screen. It is best to work with a maximised window, as all the tools will be fully available.

Restore Down button ⬚ (alternates with **Maximise**) – click this to reduce the size of your window if you want to see other programs or the Desktop behind. Several windows can be open at the same time, and the top, active, window will obscure the others. Reach them quickly by restoring down the top one. You can also move a window, by dragging, only when it is restored down.

Close button – click this to close the window. You will be reminded if you have not yet saved your work.

Scroll bars – these appear on the right and bottom of the window if the contents are too big to view. Click the arrow in the appropriate direction to move across or down the page.

Menus

Each program will have some basic options to help you organise and edit your work, as well as specific menus related to the actual program (for example, the drawing package Paint has colour and image menus that are not available when word processing). All programs have a:

- **Help** menu (offering advice on carrying out the tasks);
- **File** menu (from which to save, print or open a saved piece of work);

- **Edit** menu (for deleting or copying parts of the work: see Figure A4); and
- **View** menu (in case you need to zoom in or out to see certain areas in more detail).

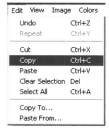

Figure A4

Dialog box

When you make a selection from a menu, you will often open a new window known as a dialog box. This may offer different 'pages' in the form of tabs that you click, and will display a range of options available either by typing in, clicking a down-facing arrow, or clicking small radio buttons or check boxes. Sometimes there are up and down arrows to increase or decrease measurements or numbers.

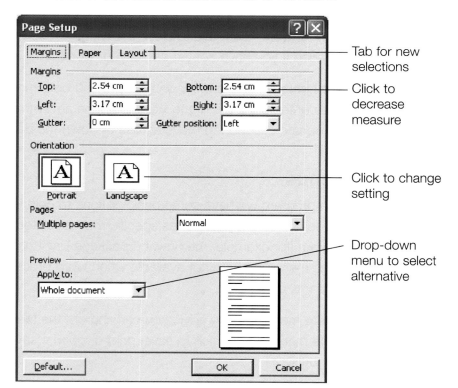

Figure A5

Help

Whenever you are stuck and cannot remember, or find out, how to do something, you should open the **Help** menu. This offers general introductions to topics via a **Contents** list, an alphabetical search through all the major topics covered via the **Index**, and a more specific keyword search using the **Search** function. Click an option in the left-hand pane and read the guidance or follow the demonstration offered on the right.

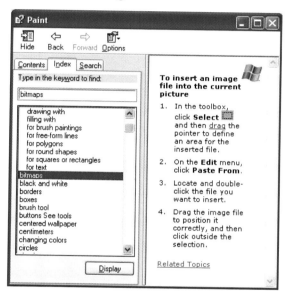

Figure A6

In most applications, you will also find a question box in the top, right-hand corner. Type in a question and press the Enter key to link up to the appropriate help text. Click the most relevant point to open the help screen.

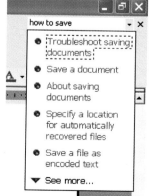

Figure A7

Index

Index

Kelkoo 90, 93–94

labels, printing 25–27
line spacing 10
links 68

McAfee anti-virus software 97
Marquee 32, 61
Maximise button 178, 179
menus 179–80
  clicking 177
  Help 179
  shortcut 178
message boards 111, 112
  see forums
Microsoft Digital Image Pro 59
Microsoft Excel 149; *see* spreadsheets
Microsoft Office XP vii
  shortcuts to 142–43, 176–77
Microsoft Word *see* word processing
Minimise button 178, 179
mistakes, correcting 4–5
mouse, using the 177–78
moving text 13–14
Mozilla 97
multiplication (on spreadsheets) 150
My Documents 7, 15, 15, 36, 176
My Pictures 33, 36, 176

Nero 37
Norton anti-virus software 97
numbering pages 12

Office XP *see* Microsoft Office XP
Outlook Express 102
  emails 105–107

page numbering 12
Paint Shop Pro 29, 59, 60
PayPal 123, 128
photographs

restoring old 59–64
  see also digital cameras; pictures
PhotoShop 29
pictures
  adding to eBay advertisement 131–32
  adding to posters (using scanners)
    53–58
  adding to text 21–23
  Desktop background 144–48
  as email attachments 108–10
  storing on CDs 38–40
  taking off Web 23, 41, 42–43
  see also digital cameras
Pinnacle Instant CD 37
pixels 28–29
Places bar 7, 7
pointer, the 4, 177
Pop-Up Stopper 97
posters, creating 53–58
PowerPoint
  creating greetings cards with 44–51
  using for posters 57–58
prices, comparing 89–95
Print Preview 8
printing 8, 9
  digital photographs 33–35
  greetings cards 51
  Web pages 75
Procreate Painter Classic 59
programs, adding or removing 141
Properties 136

radio online 76–80
  bookmarking addresses 80–82
RealOnePlayer 77
RealPlayer 77
Recycle Bin 176
Replace 13
Restore Down button 179
route-planning software 90–95
Roxio Easy CD Creator 37

We hope that this publication has been useful to you. If so, we would very much like to hear from you. Alternatively, if you feel that we could add or change anything, then please write and tell us, using the following Freepost address: Age Concern, FREEPOST CN1794, London SW16 4BR.